Excel

Revise in a Month HSC

VISUAL ARTS

Get the Results You Want!

CRAIG MALYON

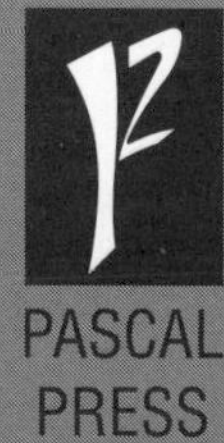

PASCAL
PRESS

Reprinted 2003, 2006, 2007, 2009, 2011
Sample HSC Examination updated for new format 2012
Reprinted 2014
Updated for syllabus changes 2021

ISBN 978 1 87708 514 7

Pascal Press
PO Box 250
Glebe NSW 2037
(02) 8585 4044
www.pascalpress.com.au

Publisher: Vivienne Joannou
Edited by May McCool and Mark Dixon
Typeset by Precision Typesetting (Barbara Nilsson)
Cover by DiZign Pty Ltd
Printed by Vivar Printing/Green Giant Press

Students
All care has been taken in compiling this study guide, but please check with your teacher or the NSW Education Standards Authority about the exact requirements of the course as they can change from year to year.

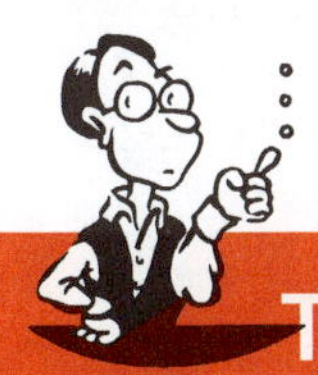

TABLE OF CONTENTS

A SUGGESTED TIME PLAN

The Artmaking section is not included in this time plan. Use the Artmaking information throughout your HSC year to help you plan, develop and submit your body of work (see page iv).

This time plan relates to the Content section of this book—Practice, the Conceptual Framework, Frames, Case Studies and the Sample HSC Examination paper—which you would use to revise in a month for your HSC written Examination paper. The time allocated is **approximately 16 hours** (plus you would need to spend some additional time revising your case studies). To revise for the HSC written Examination in a month, you would need to keep to a schedule. You may choose to follow this timetable:

Week 1	Week 2	Week 3	Week 4
Practice in Artmaking, Art Criticism and Art History Case Studies in the HSC	The Conceptual Framework—Agencies in the Artworld Case Studies in the HSC	The Frames Case Studies in the HSC	Sample HSC Examination Paper

Remember: It is important to sit the Sample HSC Examination Paper (Week 4) under exam conditions, allocating only the specified 90 minutes (plus 5 minutes reading time) to work through the paper, and about 30 minutes to review your answers.

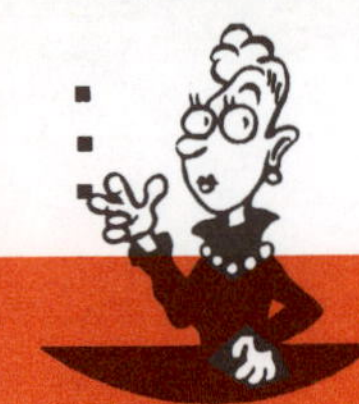

TAKE THESE STEPS TO HSC SUCCESS!

DURING THE YEAR ...

Although the focus of this book is your revision for the end-of-year HSC written Examination, we have also included a section on **artmaking and the body of work** to help you throughout the year.

Artmaking and the Body of Work

YOUR TOPIC INFO

- The first chapter in this book contains general information about **preparing your artworks** (your 'body of work') for submission in the HSC.
- This information will help you **right from the beginning of your HSC year** when you are starting to work on your own artworks.
- Use this chapter to help you **plan your body of work** in the early stages.
- It will also assist you with your focus **during the year** as you develop and shape your artworks, and will help you:
  - explore the different **expressive forms** (types of artworks in terms of style, genre and medium) you can use for your body of work
  - focus on what the **markers** (audience) will be looking for
  - **refine and resolve** your ideas
  - remember the **size, weight and other restrictions** for your artwork(s).
- The **clocks** in the top right-hand corner of each page offer **suggested reading times** for each block of information. You should, however, read and re-read this information whenever you need it.

YOUR FINAL CHECKLIST

- When your work is getting closer to completion, use the Final Checklist on page 16 to make sure your work is ready to be submitted.

TEST YOUR KNOWLEDGE

- This is a **short revision test** at the end of the Artmaking chapter to make sure you understand the important issues in preparing and submitting your artwork(s). **Check** if your **answers** are right or wrong by referring to the **answer page**.

When your artwork is complete, you can then use the remaining 'Content' chapters in this book to revise for your HSC written Examination.

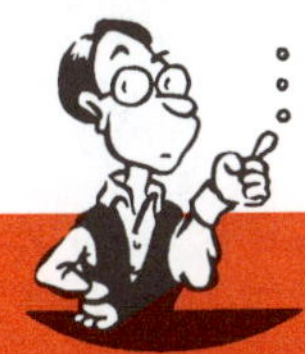

TAKE THESE STEPS TO HSC SUCCESS!

A MONTH BEFORE THE EXAM ...

CONTENT

Now you can use the rest of the book to revise your **Content** for the HSC written Examination. The Content is divided into three areas:

- **Practice in Artmaking, Art Criticism and Art History**
- **The Conceptual Framework—Agencies in the Artworld**
- **The Frames**.

There is also a section to help you revise your **case studies**, which will capitalise on your knowledge of the content of the HSC.

Step 1 YOUR TOPIC INFO

This is the **information** you will need to know to answer **examination questions**. Read through all the information provided for you for revision. An approximate **time** is allocated for each section.

The **Checkpoint** list at the end of each section will help you **double-check** your understanding of the essential information.

Step 2 TEST YOUR KNOWLEDGE

These are **short revision tests** at the end of each chapter which allow you to **recap** important information.

Check if your **answers** are right or wrong by referring to the **answer page**. This is important feedback for you.

Step 3 KEY EXAM QUESTIONS

These are **exam-style questions** that you should be able to answer in order to **prepare** for the **exam**. You should select several questions to attempt from those offered. In this section you **apply your knowledge** of the relevant section. Make sure you have **fully revised** your work in Step 1 (Your Topic Info).

Note that the **actual artworks** are not reproduced with these questions, but a reference to a book and/or website has been provided for each work. The books are common art books which you, your teacher or your library should have. If you are unable to look at a copy of the image, choose any other artwork and see if you can put together a response based on this.

Marks are allocated for each question. Always check the marks and use them as a guide for **how much to write** in your answer. These marks reflect the structure of the HSC written Examination. **Answers** and **essay guidelines** are found at the **back** of the book.

Step 4 SAMPLE HSC EXAMINATION PAPER

When you have completed all the sections, you are ready to complete the **Sample HSC Examination Paper**. Set aside the **required time** and try to do it under **exam-style conditions**.This way you will benefit most from it. **Answer guidelines** are provided for every question. **Mark** your paper to check how well you have done.

- **Tips for the HSC Examination** can be found on pages 66–73. They include comprehensive information about the structure of the exam and hints on how to answer questions and write essays.
- A **suggested time** is given for every section. Try to follow it, but it's still important you understand everything you read. If this takes you a little longer, it's worth it.
- A **week-by-week time plan** for the month is given on page iii to help you plan your study timetable.

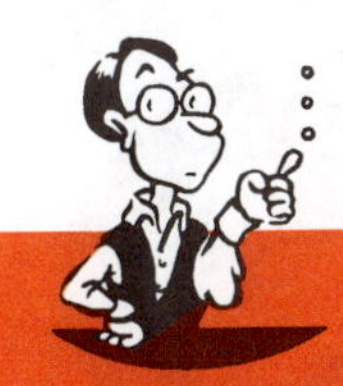

ARTMAKING IN THE HSC
The Body of Work

YOUR TOPIC INFO

What is the Body of Work?

1 **Creating artworks** might be the reason why you chose to study Visual Arts for your HSC. What you will probably have found by now is that this component is the most exciting *and* the most frustrating part. At times you will wish you had a chainsaw to destroy your work; at other times you cannot wait to show people what you have done. These **highs and lows** are part of the artmaking process.

2 Making art is like long-distance running: you can't run a marathon without any training. The Preliminary course should have offered you some training and discipline, but the HSC course offers you the chance to **explore, refine and produce artwork** that reflects who you are, what you think and what you can do. Provided you plan, experiment and remain focused you will find this a rewarding and fulfilling course.

3 So, the body of work refers to a single or multiple pieces of artwork that reflects your **artistic skills, ideas and values**. It demonstrates your commitment to artmaking and the resolution of your ideas expressed in a visual manner. You are not only expected to **produce the works**, but also think about how you can **convey meaning** through:

- the selection of **ideas** (concepts)
- the **selection and organisation** of your work (practice)
- the development of ways to **represent** both your skills and ideas.

4 This is not an easy process. Don't think you can get it done in a short amount of time. You will need to develop skills in **handling materials**, and refine and redefine your **ideas** to ensure the markers will clearly understand your intentions. You really do have to work solidly and consistently through the course.

5 Take the Australian painter **Fred Williams** as an example. He believed it was necessary to paint 200 paintings just to get the right image. Producing your own body of work is a long process which requires careful **planning and perseverance**.

Course Requirements

6 The HSC Visual Arts course is divided into two main components. Your body of work will make up **50% of the total mark**. Your BOW will either be submitted to a marking centre (this is known as **corporate marking**) or it will be marked at school by a group of markers from the NSW Education Standards Authority (**itinerant marking**).

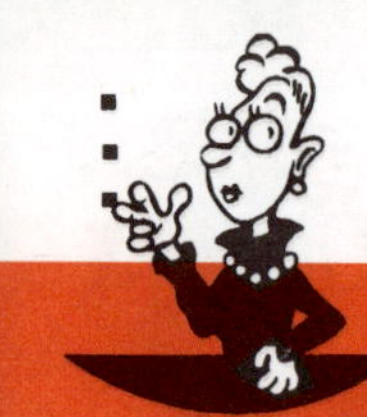

YOUR TOPIC INFO

What is the Visual Arts Process Diary?

1. The **Visual Arts Process Diary (VAPD)** is a very important part in the development of your body of work. In many ways it acts like a **map**, providing you with direction in finding out what you are interested in, and in examining **themes, media and representation**. It allows you to rough out your ideas before you produce a more refined and focused body of work. Use it to **collect, investigate and evolve** your concepts, ideas and approaches to artmaking, and to refine your techniques and skills in using particular materials.

2. The VAPD does not have to be created in the form of a book. For example, it could be collected **digitally** or **assembled in a container**. The important point is to remember that the diary provides a place to **experiment** with ideas and **assemble** objects or records that interest you. Your body of work will not miraculously spring from one single 'big idea'; it is a very organic process and it will grow from a number of ideas and experiments.

3. Your VAPD reveals the efforts you have made towards the **refinement of your artwork(s)**. It provides the space for honest **self-evaluation** of your artmaking process, as well as a place to work through any problems you are having.

4. One important fact to remember is that the VAPD is **not submitted with your body of work** for marking, although it will be retained by your school in case examiners call for the diary to assist with the marking process. This means that the proportion of time spent on the VAPD should be relative to the development of ideas and the execution of these in the body of work. So, at the beginning you will probably spend a great deal of time on the VAPD, but as you get more involved you will spend less time in experimenting and more time concentrating on the development of your body of work.

5. What **goes into the diary** is completely up to you. For example, it might be **images** that act as starting points or inspiration for your own artmaking; it may record your investigation into **materials**; or it might explore the way **artists** approach their artmaking.

CHECKPOINT:

1. *The VAPD provides the space for you to collect ideas and experiment with them in the development of your body of work.*
2. *It can be created in a variety of different forms.*
3. *It is not submitted for marking with your body of work, but it should be retained by your school.*

Sample Page of a VAPD

Your VAPD does not have to be clean and tidy. Its main function is as a diary that allows you to **make records** of discoveries, **collect stimuli** and provide a site of **experimentation**. The VAPD must be modelled in a way that works for you. It is, however, occasionally required by the HSC examiners and is always needed for your school assessment, so it should clearly reveal the process of producing your body of work.

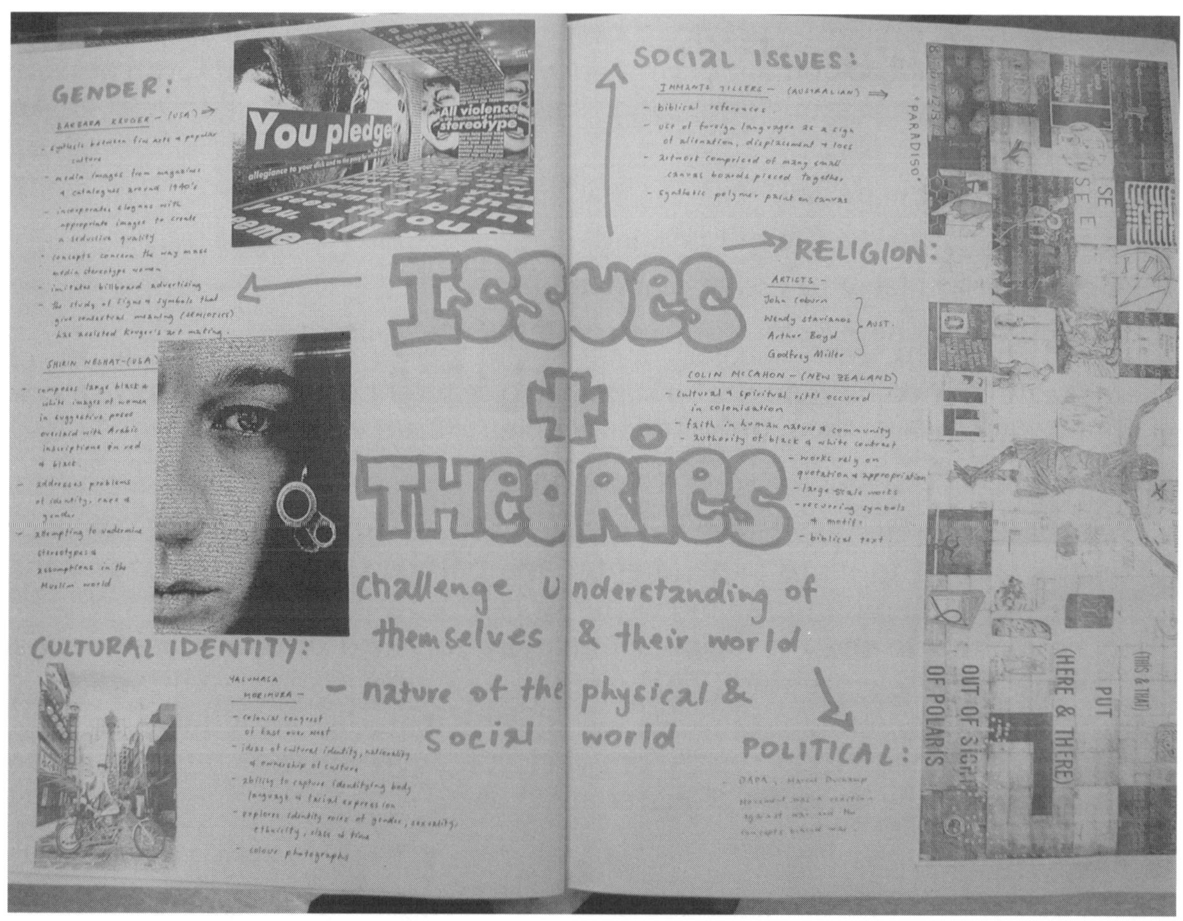

Sample VAPD page by a student, Anjuli Maniam

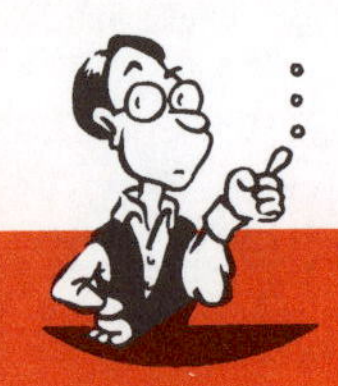

ARTMAKING IN THE HSC
The Expressive Forms

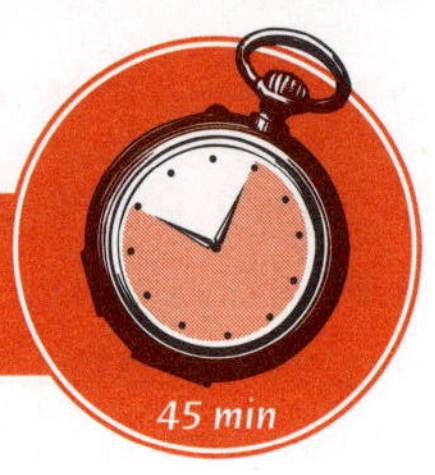

YOUR TOPIC INFO

What are the Expressive Forms?

Expressive forms can be considered as **media areas** which are available for your artmaking. These categories provide a basis for artmaking and you may nominate to use them in the development of your body of work. The different forms provide a wide scope for your artmaking. When selecting your expressive form(s), make sure you consider:

- the **expense** of materials
- your **expertise** in the use of materials
- **equipment** available to you at school and at home
- the **appropriateness** of the form to communicate your ideas.

There are different **requirements** for submitting different types of expressive forms in your body of work. Here are some guidelines to help you.

1. **Drawing**
   Approaches to this expressive form range greatly from **traditional forms** of representation to more **experimental approaches** that seek to extend the aesthetic conditions of drawing as an expressive form. Drawing doesn't have to be limited to the use of pencil: exploration into **different materials** is encouraged. The more traditional methods use pencils and pastels, while the experimental works might involve such diverse materials as bitumen paper or packing cardboard. To succeed in drawing, your work needs to reflect **skill and innovation** in the handling of materials.

2. **Painting**
   This is one of the **dominant expressive forms** in HSC Visual Arts, as it is in the artworld itself. There is a broad range of possible approaches to painting which reflects the diverse language of this medium. It is worth familiarising yourself with **different paint media**, such as oils, acrylics, enamels, encaustic and tempera. Each provides a different effect and requires different skills. Make sure you give yourself plenty of time for experimentation. Do some **research** into artists who have used your chosen media and learn from their approaches. Remember that both **figuration and abstraction** are difficult genres that require lots of work to perfect. Importantly, you must ensure that **any painting you submit is dry** on the submission date. If you are using oil paints and glazes, you must give yourself plenty of time for your work to dry before you pack it up. Many

artworks in competitions have been spoiled due to poor management of time. The Archibald Prize does not allow wet paintings to be submitted, and neither does the NSW Education Standards Authority.

3 Photomedia

The popularity of photographic images in social media has seen a rapid evolution in style, genre and approaches to photo-based artworks. This expressive form allows for a diverse range of approaches associated with photography ranging from digital to analog, camera and non-camera photography. The availability of different printing papers for digital printing has extended the creative potential to producing different outcomes using matte, semi-gloss or gloss paper. The innovations within apps and programs have allowed for more innovative production in this expressive form.

4 Printmaking

The expressive form encapulates tradtional media such as serigraphy, block and intaglio printing, as well as more experimental forms such as collagraph and hybrid forms that incorporate digital technology in printing or the etching of the plate. It is not necessary to submit the **entire edition** of a work. However, if this demonstrates a resolution of your practical approach to printmaking, then submit the edition. There is also no need to hand in the **plate** with the image. Lino blocks and etching plates do not need to be submitted unless they are to be considered as artworks in their own right.

5 Graphic Design

This relates to design submissions such as posters, advertising campaigns, desktop publishing and multimedia. The **aesthetic power** of the work and its **intended function** are the important elements. Often a graphic design submission can be accompanied with a **design brief** to explain the intentions of the work and outline the targeted users for the designs. The range of submission is broad and includes graphic novels, movie character illustrations, posters, and ID and logo designs.

6 Time-based Forms

This expressive form includes video, interactive, animated digital and documentary works you must make sure that the submitted video **does not run over six minutes**. In your credits, try to include the software used, music credits and reference to any sourced imagery used. This assists the markers in the judgement of your work. Ensure the submitted copy has no flaws in the sound or image quality, and always make sure you **make a copy** and keep it in a safe place as a precaution. **acknowledging copyright** is essential. If you have copied any sound or images from other sources, these must be credited. Ask your teacher for more information, or refer to the HSC Visual Arts syllabus.

7 Sculpture

The forms that are submitted within sculpture are **rich and diverse**, reflecting a number of approaches to producing the artworks and the development of ideas. Sculpture can take **many forms**, including carving, modelling and assemblage, and can reflect the current contemporary practices of installation work, site-specific works and performance. If you are submitting a sculpture, you need to think about the way the work is **constructed**. Will it make it to the marking centre in one piece? Is it within the **size restriction** of one cubic metre and **weight restriction** of 34.4 kg? Note that installation, site-specific or performance works can be submitted in alternative ways for marking—see Documented forms.

8 Ceramics

There are a wide variety of ceramic forms and techniques: **hand-building, slip-casting and thrown pots** are all aspects of ceramics. In this expressive form it is worth noting the importance of giving yourself **plenty of time** to work on your ceramics and fire them. It is a good idea to document your **stages of development** in ceramics to ensure that, if a mishap occurs in transportation, you have a visual record of your work. Both sculptural ceramic forms and vessels or pots can be submitted.

9 Textiles and fibres

This is very much like working in the tradition of sculpture but with the use of **materials and fabrics**. It is a beguiling expressive form that requires a lot of patience and skill, since it is a very labour-intensive process. Yet the final works can reflect refinement and experimentation in the handling of materials, providing good results for certain students. It might look easy, but don't be fooled into thinking it is.

10 Designed objects and environments

A majority of these submissions are **wearables** (such as jewellery) but the form(s) also include(s) **architectural models** and **industrial designs**. There is a wide range of possibilities for this category. Wearables are sculptural forms suited to the living body, *not* everyday functional clothing. For example, you might design a set of costumes for the characters in a play. Note that the syllabus specifically says that you should *not* submit a mannequin for clothing designs. If you wish to demonstrate how the garment looks on the human form, you can take photographs. Make sure that the photographs **complement** the garment, rather than hinder its presentation. They should demonstrate the significance of the 'art wear' on the human form. It is extremely important to make sure that **no sewing needles** are left in the work and that sharp edges are filed down.

11 Collection of works

As the title suggests, this area allows you to submit within a variety of expressive forms, for example, a drawing, print and sculpture. It offers you a range of experiences in the development of your body of work. Importantly, though, in this category your body of work **is only as good as your weakest work** so it is worth selecting the better works that convey the concepts you are exploring and show your skills in artmaking. The separate pieces of work may be interrelated or may be quite different, but if the works are very different and they do not strengthen the concept you are attempting to relay to the audience, then you may need to rethink your approach. If you started your artworks in one category and then expanded your investigations into other media—and all the works are equally strong in their technical resolution and conceptual meaning—then collection of works might be the category for you.

12 Documented forms

This expressive form relates to artworks or events that **cannot be submitted**. Examples include artworks which are **temporal** (lasting only a short amount of time, e.g. works containing fire, water, ice, living materials, decaying or decomposing objects), **performances** and art forms that are so far **over the size or weight restrictions** they can only be documented and the record of the work submitted. Your submisison may be a site specific work this type of work relates and involves specific spaces much like some of the installations in Sculpture by the Sea. It important in this form to ensure that the way you present the **visual information** provides the best account of the actual work. You can submit a series of **photographs**, a **film** or video, or a **digital work**. It is important to ensure that, whatever way you choose to document your work, the **form of documentation** best represents your ideas and use of materials.

TIPS

- For information on size and weight restrictions, see pages 12–15.
- Glass or rigid plastic should not be used for mounting. A simple box mount on mount board is sufficient, allowing the marker to scrutinise your work in detail if needed.

CHECKPOINT:

1. *Choose an expressive form you are good at using and which you enjoy using.*
2. *Each expressive form has certain requirements for submission. Make sure you are familiar with them. Consult your teacher and the HSC Visual Arts syllabus.*
3. *Make sure you have looked into the cost of materials and the equipment you will need to use in preparing your body of work.*

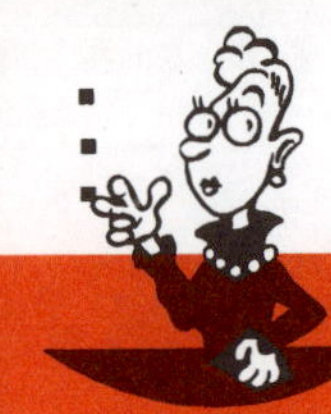

ARTMAKING IN THE HSC
Working on the Body of Work

YOUR TOPIC INFO

Getting Started

1. Firstly, think about what **themes or ideas** you wish to explore.
2. Identify what **you are good at**, i.e. recognise your skills in particular expressive forms.
3. Examine how **other artists** have used materials and solved issues through their artworks.
4. Use your VAPD as the basis of **documenting your progress** and collecting materials, ideas, information about artists and anything else that may assist you in your artmaking.
5. A **concept map** is a good way of mapping out your body of work and how you would like to develop it. Below is a concept map summarising main points about the body of work.

Body of Work

Restrictions
Are there restrictions in what you can do for the BOW in terms of size, weight or duration?

Cost
How much will the **processes and materials** cost to produce your artworks? Can you afford them?

Innovation
How can you be **unique?** Can you use your ideas and handle the material in an **original manner**?

Artists
Which artists have you studied who interest you? How do they use their **ideas and materials** in their artmaking?

Critical assessment
Are you working in partnership with your teacher who can give you help, advice and support? Your friends and peers will also provide **valuable assessment** during the development of your BOW.

Themes and issues
Have you selected an area that is **interesting** to you? It's easier if you work with a theme that reflects your interests or tells the audience something about you and your understanding of visual art.

Technical skill and handling of materials
Have you selected an **expressive form** that can show off your skills as an artist? Have you developed competency in the selected form?

Time frame and time management
How much time do you have before the BOW is due for submission? How will you plan your **time** so you don't leave it until the last minute?

Elements to Consider in the Body of Work

6 In making your body of work you need to consider a number of elements to ensure that a **coherent resolution** in your ideas and your use of materials is conveyed to the markers. Consider these points in your artmaking:

- Ensure that the BOW reflects a development from **intuitive exploration** of subject matter to a more **intentional communication of ideas**.
- Demonstrate an obvious **development** from the experimentation that appears in your VAPD to a **resolved final product** in your BOW.
- Realise that working on your BOW is a process of **constant refinement**. Don't just be happy with initial ideas: work towards a greater resolution of your concepts and technical skills.
- The start of your BOW is a **journey in artmaking** where the possibilities are infinite. You will need to distill these experiences into the BOW.
- You need to be **selective** with your treatment of subject matter and in constructing your BOW. You cannot include every idea you have.
- The BOW should be **multilayered in meaning** so it can be interpreted in different ways by different people, but it still should have a **message** to convey which is clear and precise.
- Ensure there is technical refinement in your handling of materials. Demonstrate your **skill and expertise** in the selection and use of the expressive form(s) employed to construct your BOW.
- Your BOW should reveal a **connection** between your ideas and your use of materials. Why have you chosen a particular expressive form to demonstrate your idea? Will this connection be clear to the marker?
- Think of yourself as both an **artist** and a **curator.** Your BOW is like an exhibition organised by a curator to convey ideas and show artistic techniques. This is best done through **careful selection** of works, so be very critical of your own selection. Ensure it best represents your ideas and your use of materials. Don't add pieces to your collection unless they support your theme and show consistency.
- As you come to understand the **Conceptual Framework** and the **Frames**, you will find them very useful in your artmaking. The Conceptual Framework will help you to 'map out' the artmaking process (starting with yourself as 'artist'), while the Frames will help you identify and focus your ideas.

CHECKPOINT:

1. *Plan your body of work thoroughly. Make sure you develop your themes and issues in your work, and that your intention is clear.*
2. *Use techniques such as concept maps to explore possibilities for your body of work.*
3. *Your body of work should show how you have carefully selected and refined your ideas.*
4. *Try to make it clear why you have chosen a particular expressive form to represent your ideas.*

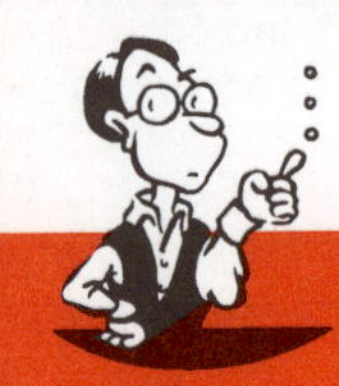

ARTMAKING IN THE HSC
Marking the Body of Work

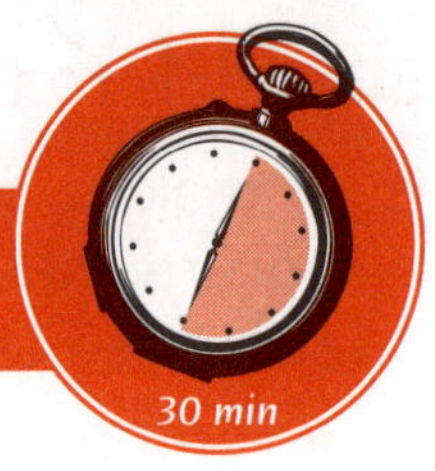

YOUR TOPIC INFO

Marking Criteria

1 There are two main criteria used in the marking of the body of work. They are:
- your **technical resolution** in the handling of your chosen media
- the **conceptual strength and meaning** of the work(s).

Note that in your **internal** (school) assessment, you will be assessed on the other outcomes listed in the syllabus.

2 It is the combination of these two criteria which will effectively shape your body of work. It is helpful to use them to judge the success of **your own artmaking**. Often students find it hard to look at their own work in a **critical manner**. Your teachers and peers will offer advice, but it is worth attempting to evaluate your body of work for yourself.

3 **Technical resolution**
- The technical resolution refers to the **skills in handling the material** demonstrated in the work, and the approach to using the medium which is displayed.
- The markers will review and scrutinise the way you have used materials and how effectively you have **developed** your BOW through the selected expressive form(s). They will be looking for **competency** in the handling of materials and **innovation** in techniques.

TIPS

- At the end of the Preliminary course, carefully select expressive forms in artmaking that **you are good at** so you will have no difficulty in manipulating the medium and developing new ways of using it. Discuss this with your teacher for guidance in choosing your form. If you use materials and a medium you enjoy using, you are more likely to **experiment** and develop a **sophisticated knowledge** in handling them.
- Remember that good artworks are not just invented: they are the product of careful **planning, development** of skills and a lot of **experimentation**.
- Identify the **specifications** for your choice of art form set by the NSW Education Standards Authority (NESA), and ensure your body of work fits within them. You can look up the specifications in the syllabus which can be found on the NESA website (www.educationstandards.nsw.edu.au) or by asking your teacher.
- It is a good idea to align your own artmaking experimentation with a **particular artist or style** to assist in developing your own work.
- Use your **VAPD** to support the development of your body of work.

4 **Conceptual strength and meaning**

- This relates to the message you are conveying in your artwork and how **clear and complex** it is.
- It refers to how well your **thoughts, ideas and concepts** are being explored and conveyed.

TIPS

- Make sure you have a good understanding of the **practice** of visual arts and how it informs artmaking.
- Your work should reflect your understanding of the three core areas of study for HSC Visual Arts: **Practice, Conceptual Framework** and **the Frames**.
- Examine **authentic concerns and concepts** that are relevant to your world.
- Constantly look to **evolve and refine your ideas** to ensure that your body of work is **resolved** in its artistic intention.
- Think of your body of work as a **book** which can be read in a visual manner. Just as books need to communicate their ideas clearly to the reader, so your artwork needs to **communicate its ideas** clearly to the marker.
- Develop **personal signs and symbols** that reflect your own approach to artmaking. You can construct both public and private symbols that enrich the overall meaning of the work.
- Identify **strategies** and **philosophies** which artists you have studied have employed in the development of artworks. Think about how these artists have represented their ideas, themes and issues.
- Trace **concepts and theories** from artists, historians and critics and use these to strengthen your own ideas.

The Artist as Curator

5 Your BOW will need to be constructed in a manner that reflects the strengths of both the techniques and concepts in the work. To do this, you will effectively take on the role of a curator who selects the best aspects of artworks for an exhibition—your BOW is that exhibition. A curator carefully selects works for an exhibition for a particular purpose. So when you choose the works to include, it is important to look at the how you use a single piece or a series to best represent your **time, energy** and **commitment**. How well do they communicate the ideas your have been involved in exploring? How well do they show your handling of materials used in the artmaking process?

It is also worth reviewing the stated outcomes of artmaking which appear in the HSC Visual Arts syllabus.

CHECKPOINT:

1. *Two key criteria for marking a body of work are 'technical resolution' and 'conceptual strength and meaning'.*
2. *These two areas need to work together to shape your body of work.*
3. *The body of work is not just a portfolio of artworks you have produced. It must be developed according to these two criteria.*

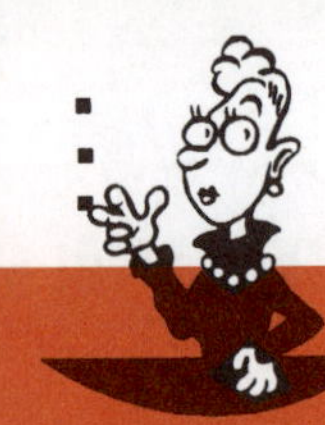

ARTMAKING IN THE HSC
Submitting the Body of Work

YOUR TOPIC INFO

Points to Consider

1. Ensure that you submit a body of work which **complies with all the criteria** outlined by the NESA.
2. Conditions such as **restrictions in size and weight** need to be followed. These apply to the **artwork and its packaging together**, *not* just the artwork itself. Ignoring these conditions means your submission could be penalised.
3. It important that you are aware of the **restrictions and guidelines** set for the submission of your body of work. These are in the HSC Visual Arts syllabus which can be found on the NSW Education Standards Authority website.
4. The **maximum weight** for your body of work is **35 kg, including the packaging**. Don't go over this weight restriction.

Surface Area: Two Square Metres

5. The maximum **surface area** for a **two-dimensional** body of work is **six square metres (6 m^2)** with individual works being no bigger than two square metres, unless the artwork is rolled or hinged together. Surface area is calculated as **height × width**. Each of the following items is two square metres.

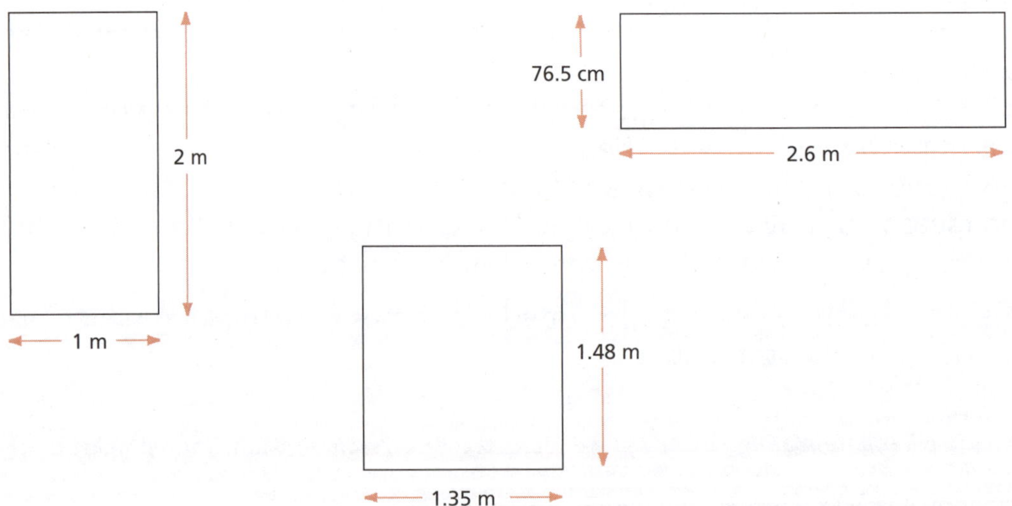

Note: *Diagrams are not to scale and are intended as a guide only.*

Reference table for two square metres of a flat surface

50 cm x 4 m	1.1 m x 1.81 m	2.3 m x 86.5 cm
60 cm x 3.33 m	1.2 m x 1.66 m	2.4 m x 83 cm
70 cm x 2.85 m	1.3 m x 1.53 m	2.6 m x 76.5 cm
80 cm x 2.5 m	2 m x 1 m	2.8 m x 71 cm
90 cm x 2.22 m	2.1 m x 95 cm	3 m x 66.5 cm
1 m x 2 m	2.2 m x 90 cm	5 m x 40 cm

Note: measurements are rounded off to the nearest centimetre.

Volumetric Dimension: One Cubic Metre

6 The maximum **volumetric dimension** for a three-dimensional body of work is **one cubic metre (1 m^3)**. Volumetric dimension is calculated as height × width × depth. Each of the following items is one cubic metre.

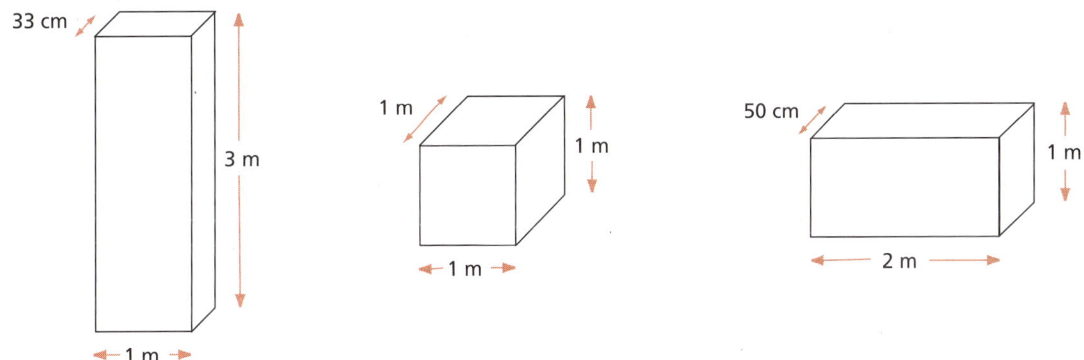

Note: *Diagrams are not to scale and are intended as a guide only.*

7 In sculptural works, the **negative space** is included in the limitation of one cubic metre when the body of work is displayed. This means that the armatures that protrude far from the base will be measured in terms of the volume of negative space as well as solid space.

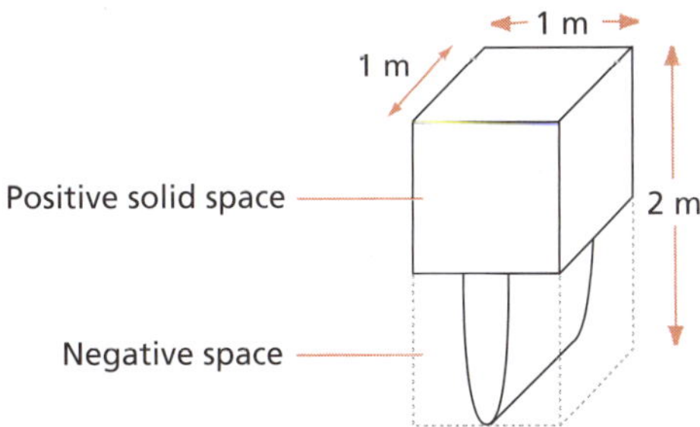

The negative space in this sculpture would be considered part of the complete volume of the artwork, making it over the size limit.

8 If your body of work includes both two-dimensional and three-dimensional works, the **total volume measurement** is used, which includes any **space** between the works. Do not just calculate the two-dimensional surface area plus the three-dimensional volume. This is particularly relevant for many submissions in the Collection of Works category. You need to carefully consider how the works will be set up for marking, and provide the markers with specific instructions on how to set up the works so the maximum volume is not exceeded. So don't forget —**space between the works** is included in your overall volume measurement.

Packing up the Body of Work

9 You have just spent hundreds of hours on your body of work, racked your brain to come up with an original and highly sophisticated idea, and poured in blood, sweat and tears to get it to look just right. The last thing you want to do is ruin this all by packing your work poorly. Here are some guidelines:

- **Plan now** how you will get your artwork to the markers. If your school is being **itinerantly marked** (where the markers come to your school), ensure that it will be stored in a safe place at school.
- Your teacher will arrange a time for you to sign the **certification paperwork** required by the NESA. This is a signed statement which declares that the body of work is all your own work, and it must be witnessed by your teacher. However, *you* are responsible for **packaging** your body of work so it can be safely transported to the marking centre. Take time to arrange this: bubble wrap, masking tape, labels and any other materials you need.
- Ensure that if your artwork needs **special packaging** you have time to do this.
- If the if the work need to be **arranged in a special way**, make sure instructions are on the back. It is often a good idea to attach a **photograph** of how you would like the work assembled to the back of one of the works.
- Remember that the **size and weight restrictions** apply to the BOW when it is **wrapped** and not before. It is worth having a tape measure, calculator and scales to make final checks before sending it off to the examiners.

TIPS

- Remember the **size and weight restrictions** outlined by the NESA. The weight restriction applies to the **packaging** as well as the work itself. Ask your teacher, or refer to the Visual Arts syllabus or the NESA website for further instructions.
- If there are any **sharp edges** or **protruding parts** on the work that could harm people who pick it up, it will be considered dangerous and not meet the conditions outlined by NESA. Think about how you can blunt the edges and make the work easier to handle. And *never*, under any circumstances, use hypodermic syringes, needles, bodily secretions or blood products!

- If you have an **electrical component** which requires the work to be plugged in, it must have a **compliance certificate** from an electrician.
- Make sure you have written down the correct **student and school numbers** on the identification label.
- Be realistic about how the markers will **set up** your body of work. If it is extremely complex, without any instructions or support, it may cause problems for the markers. Supplying **photographs** showing how it should be assembled will be helpful to the markers.
- Special arrangements need to be made for a collection of work submission as the duration of video work (if submitted) can only be three minutes.
- Always check the NESA website to ensure you are aware of any changes made in terms of submission restrictions.

CHECKPOINT:

1. *Your body of work must comply with all the criteria specified by the NSW Education Standards Authority. Make sure you know what these are.*
2. *Size and weight restrictions include the packaging of your work.*
3. *For three-dimensional works, you must include the negative space as part of the total volume of the work.*
4. *For bodies of work which include both two-dimensional and three-dimensional works, the total volume includes any space between the works.*

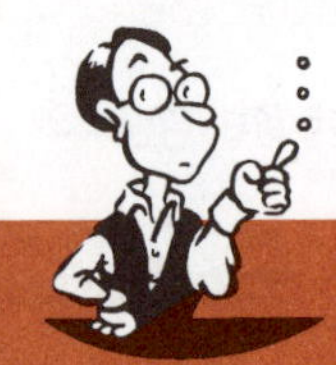

ARTMAKING IN THE HSC

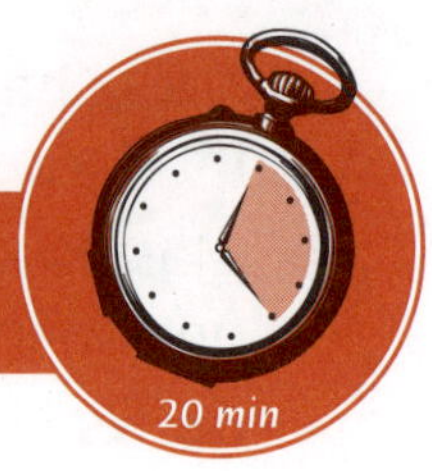

YOUR FINAL CHECKLIST

☐ **Do you know the submission date for your body of work?**
You can find this on the NESA website: www.educationstandards.nsw.edu.au

☐ **Look over your body of work. Have you fully resolved the handling of materials and media?**
Only you can honestly answer this, but use the information about 'technical resolution' and 'conceptual strength and meaning' on pages 10–11, and ask people such as your teacher, friends and family if they understand your intentions and appreciate how you handled the materials for your work(s).

☐ **Does your work communicate its intended message clearly to an audience?**
Ask a wide cross-section of people to ensure the work conveys the intended ideas and concepts. Examine how other artists have conveyed their ideas through specific connections and the establishment of sign systems. If you find that you need to explain the work to people and they still have trouble grasping the concept(s), you may need to refine your work. Your teacher should be the first person you discuss this with.

☐ **Are there any weak components in the body of work?**
If there are, you might want to consider if they are really necessary for inclusion. It pays to be completely honest with yourself. If there are problems with the work, don't ignore them, but instead work upon a resolution. If you're tired of the work, leave it for a brief period and return to it later. A break should help you look at it with fresh eyes.

☐ **Would your body of work benefit from a specific title or an artist's statement to help the marker understand your intentions?**
For some works, this can assist the marker's understanding. For other artworks, however, it limits the potential meaning(s) that can be associated with the work.

☐ **Are you certain that your work is compliant with the rules and specifications outlined by the NESA?**
Ask your teacher for clarification or visit the NESA website and view the HSC Visual Arts syllabus. Acknowledge this as your own responsibility and make sure you know everything you have to before the submission date.

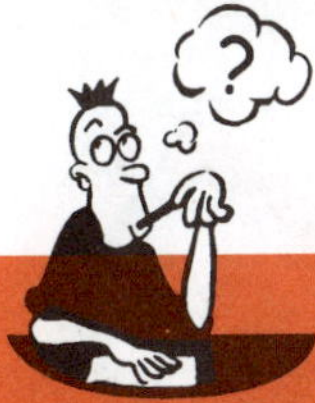

ARTMAKING IN THE HSC

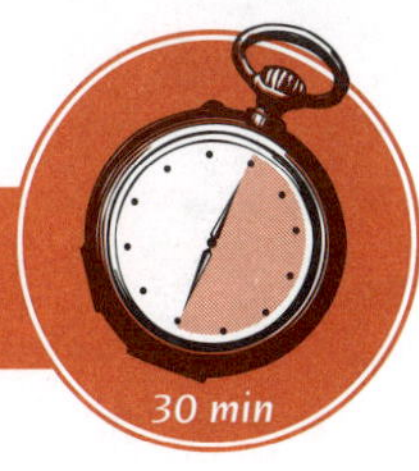

TEST YOUR KNOWLEDGE

1. What is your understanding of a body of work (BOW)?

2. Explain what the concept of 'technical resolution' in a BOW means to you.

3. How can 'conceptual strength and meaning' be conveyed in a BOW?

4. What is an expressive form?

5. What is the maximum weight allowed for a BOW when packed up?

6. What is the maximum surface area allowed for a two-dimensional BOW when packed up?

7. What is the maximum volume allowed for a three-dimensional BOW when displayed for marking?

8. What things should you avoid putting in your BOW which would make it dangerous for a marker to handle?

9. What percentage of your HSC Visual Arts mark is the BOW worth?

10. What is the role of a Visual Arts Process Diary?

☞ *Answers on pages 80–81*

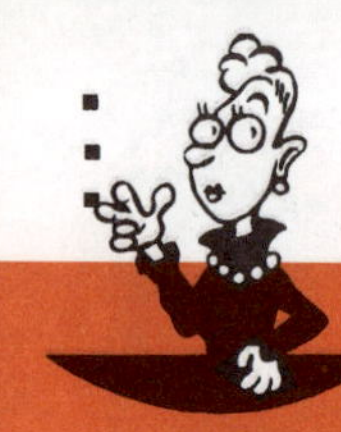

PRACTICE IN ARTMAKING, ART CRITICISM & ART HISTORY
Components of the HSC Content

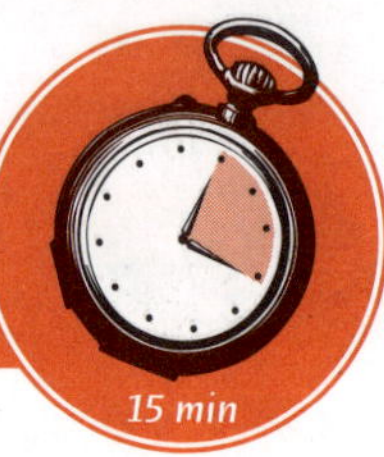

YOUR TOPIC INFO

What is the HSC 'Content'?

1. The **content for study** in HSC Visual Arts is divided into three components:
   - Practice in Artmaking, Art Criticism and Art History
   - The Conceptual Framework—Agencies in the Artworld
   - The Frames.

2. It is important to know how to use these three components as the basis for **research and investigation**.

3. The HSC content asks you to make connections and develop an understanding of the **different relationships** that exist within the visual arts. Although this may seem challenging, in many ways it offers a **structured approach** to studying and responding to artworks and designs.

4. The **relationship** between the Practice, Conceptual Framework and Frames areas is **interwoven**, as shown below. You need to understand each of these areas thoroughly—and also understand how they **work together**—to do well in your exam.

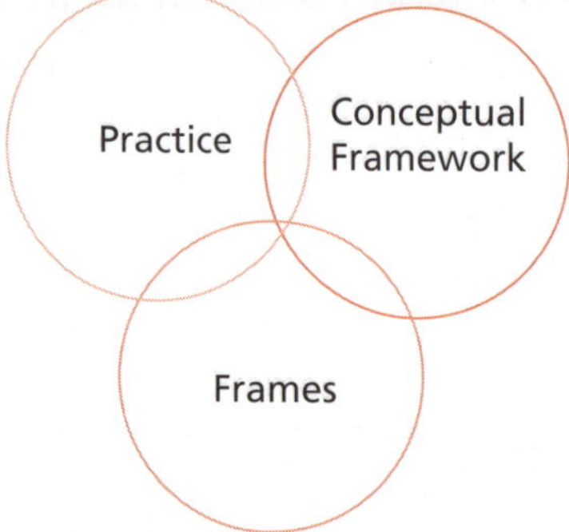

For more information on the **structure of the HSC written Examination paper**, see pages 66–73.

CHECKPOINT:
1. *There are three areas of core content you need to be familiar with: Practice, Conceptual Framework and Frames.*
2. *All of these areas will be tested in the HSC written Examination paper.*

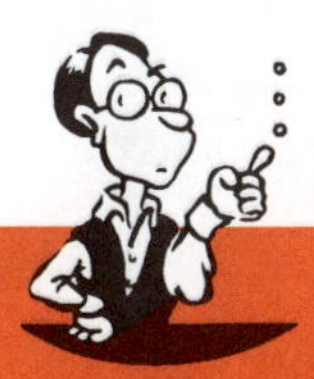

PRACTICE IN ARTMAKING, ART CRITICISM & ART HISTORY

Identifying Practice in the Visual Arts

YOUR TOPIC INFO

Key Areas within the Practice Component

1. In the Practice area of content, you will need to identify and explore **three key areas**:
   - artmaking
   - art criticism
   - art history.

2. As the word suggests, the Practice component deals with the **'doing'** of things in the world of art. It refers to **activities or actions** within visual arts. The Practice area seeks to **outline and evaluate** key aspects within the visual arts and examine how knowledge about artworks and artists can develop through **historical and critical study**.

3. This component differentiates the significant activities of **artmaking, criticism** and **historical** studies that can shape our perceptions of the visual arts. By studying the practices of people involved in the artworld, you come to recognise how **artists**, **historians** and **critics** can bring meaning to art and provide ways of interpreting it. As you become more familiar with these practices, you will be more able to judge and assess your own **body of work** as well as the works of other artists in your **case studies**.

4. The Practice component offers the **basic building blocks** within the visual arts. Developing your knowledge of this core content will ensure a greater success in all aspects of HSC Visual Arts.

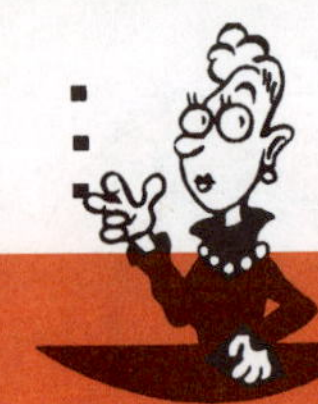

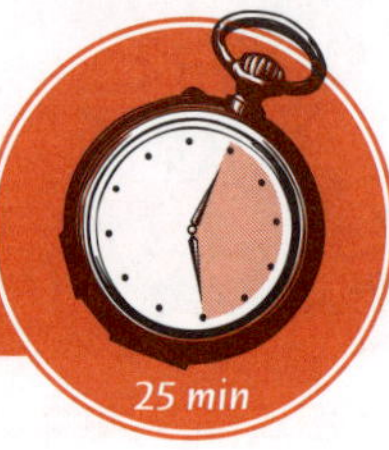

YOUR TOPIC INFO

What is Artmaking Practice?

1. The **artmaking** part of the Practice component relates to both your own **practical experiences** in the production of your body of work, and recognising the **approaches and intentions of artists** you have studied.

2. It asks you to consider all the things that might be important in the **production of an artwork**. These include:
   - treatment and use of materials
   - representation of thoughts, feelings and experiences
   - stylistic innovations
   - the artist's intention and philosophy
   - emerging technologies
   - personal symbols and signs
   - ideas and concepts.

Strategies, Meanings and Interpretations

3. Within every artwork there are **layers of meaning**. An artist will hide or expose meaning at their own discretion. This highlights the importance of the relationship between the **artwork and the audience**, and how artists orchestrate this relationship in their artmaking. Both within your own artmaking and in the study of other artworks, you will become aware of the different **strategies and intentions** that each artist develops.

4. You will also become conscious of how artists **interpret the world** through their art. These interpretations are shaped through the **technical resolution** and the **conceptual strength and meaning** in their artworks (see pages 9–11 for discussion of these concepts). Artmaking is not a result of artists just making art by themselves. Rather, the complex connections that are established between **artists and their worlds**, and between **audiences** (including critics and historians) **and artworks**, are crucial in how artwork is produced.

Artmaking in the HSC Written Examination

5. In the HSC written Examination paper you may be asked to investigate artists' **intentions and approaches** to the production of artworks. You will need to

identify differing **purposes and methods** of artmaking and discuss the governing features which may affect the production of an artwork.

Artmaking within the Visual Arts

6 The following mindmap shows a summary of different aspects of the **practice of artmaking**. These are the issues you should consider when you study the work of other artists, and also in your own artmaking practice.

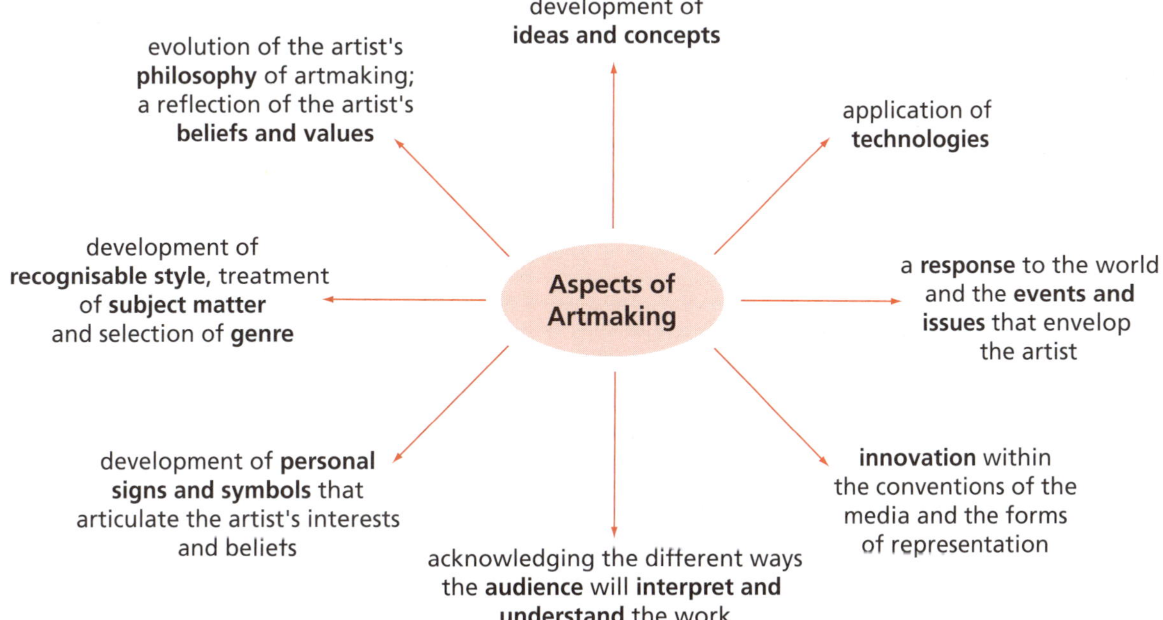

CHECKPOINT:

1. *The artmaking area of the Practice component deals with both your own practical experiences as you work on your artworks, and analysing the approaches and intentions of artists you study.*
2. *There are many factors which go into the production of an artwork. You will need to be able to identify these in the HSC written Examination.*

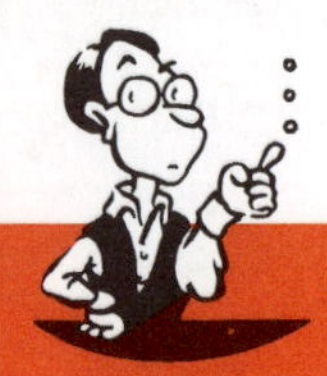

PRACTICE IN ARTMAKING, ART CRITICISM & ART HISTORY
Art Criticism

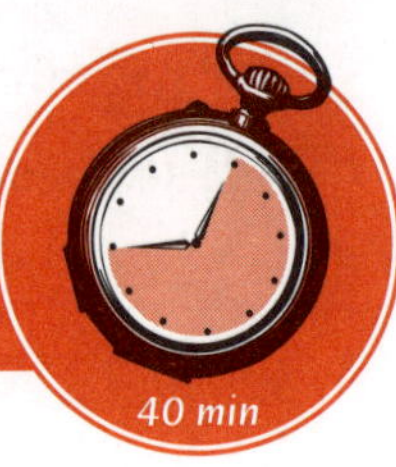

YOUR TOPIC INFO

What is the Role of the Art Critic?

1 **Art criticism** is, in itself, a **creative activity** that aims to map the ways in which different meanings are represented in artworks. The objective of the critic is to **clarify and assess**:
- the **qualities** of an artwork
- how an artist **develops and produces** art
- how the **audience** may **view, understand** and **appreciate** the artwork.

2 The critic could be thought of as a **navigator** who offers a way of reading a map about the visual arts. Art criticism **examines, evaluates** and **explains** the significance of artworks and attempts to **decipher meaning** for an audience.

3 A **good art critic** will:
- provide a **comprehensive account** of the artwork in terms of its theme, style, form of representation and use of technology for an audience
- read the artwork in terms of its **visual language**—that is, its **conceptual strength and meaning** as well as its **technical resolution**
- evaluate and explain what is **significant** in an artwork
- establish **relevance** between the **artwork and the audience**
- show an audience how to look at an artwork and find **meaning(s)** in it
- establish a **presence of authority** within the artwork, ie. emphasise the aspects of the artwork which make it so distinctive and unique
- carefully select and **synthesise** (merge or blend) **ideas and values** to make an informed statement about the artwork
- highlight the **codes and conventions** that can be found in the work.

Types of Critical Judgement

4 According to Edmund Burke Feldman in his book *Varieties of Visual Experience* (Abrams, New York, 1992), there are three types of **critical judgements** used by critics within visual arts to investigate artworks and artists.
- **Formal judgement** deals with the **structural elements** of the artwork.
- **Expressivist judgement** deals with the **subjective and expressive qualities** of the work.
- **Instrumentalist judgement** uses the idea that the artwork expresses a particular **ideology** that envelops artist and artwork. This kind of criticism examines the **cultural and postmodern** aspects of the artwork.

Types of Critics

5 **Conservative Critics**

- Conservative critics take a **conventional approach** to discussing art.
- They use **classical and traditional aesthetic conventions** to make their judgements about artworks.
- They are primarily concerned with the **structural** (formal and design elements) and **subjective** (personal) **qualities** in an artwork and acknowledge the importance of the **formal qualities** found in an artwork.
- Conservative critics believe that an artwork maintains an **'inner beauty'** and that the artwork should **speak for itself**.

6 **Radical Critics**

- Radical criticism provides accounts of artworks that **differ** from those offered by more traditional critics.
- Many radical critics examine **how meaning is constructed** and how the meaning of an artwork may differ depending on **who is looking at the artwork**. For instance, a **feminist art critic** may view Picasso's painting *Les Demoiselles d'Avignon* (1907) quite differently to a more conservative critic.
- The radical critic attempts to **question the conventions and codes** within art, and reviews them in terms of their **cultural and postmodern significance**.

Studying Art Criticism

7 As your study of the visual arts becomes more detailed, your knowledge and skills in art criticism will increase. You will learn how to **interrogate, evaluate and construct meanings** in artworks using your knowledge of practice, conceptual framework and frames in art. You need to learn about **art critics' techniques** and how you can apply them in your own writing.

8 Your **criticism** about art should:

- involve more than **personal judgements**
- clearly describe the **effectiveness** of an artwork
- assess an artwork **in relation to the world**, not as an isolated piece of work
- display your **specialised knowledge** of the visual arts.

Art Criticism in the HSC Written Examination

9 In the HSC written Examination paper you will be required to demonstrate your **ability as a critic** when writing about artworks. Your interpretation of both the question asked in the examination and the artists/artworks/critics/historians you discuss in your response is dependent on your ability to understand both the question and works soundly.

The Practice of Art Criticism

10 The following mindmap shows a summary of different aspects of the **practice of art criticism**.

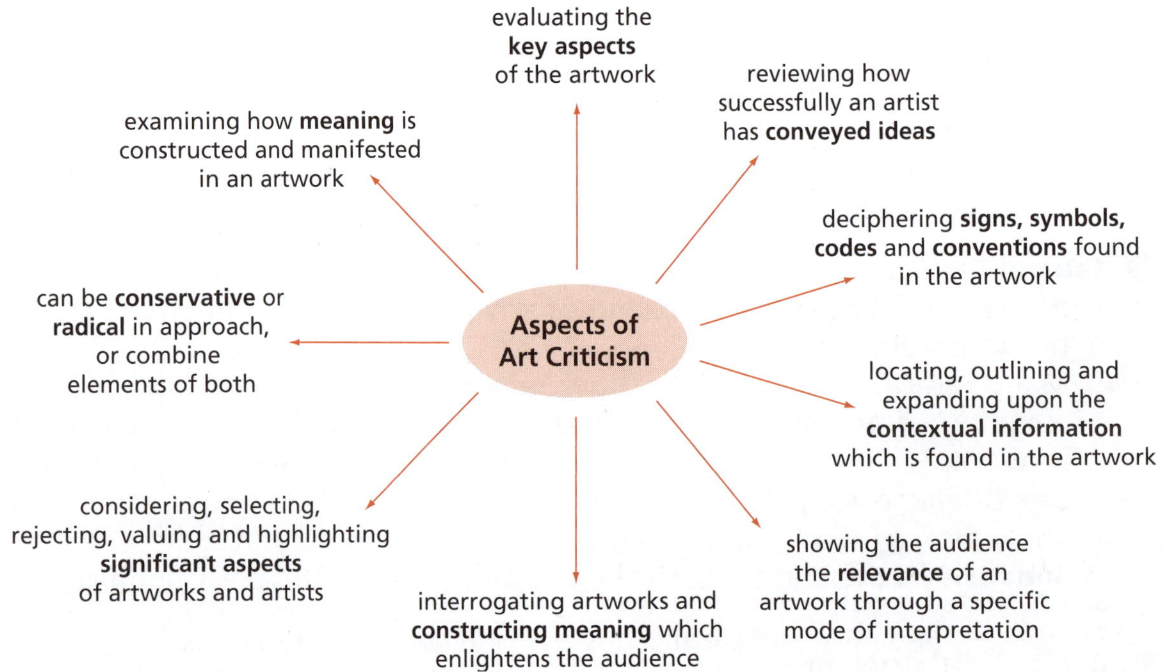

CHECKPOINT:

1. *The art criticism area of the Practice component deals with the way art critics approach their assessments of artwork.*
2. *Art criticism examines, evaluates and explains artworks for an audience. The art critic is like a bridge between the audience and the artist/artwork.*
3. *The three types of critical judgement (as identified by Edmund Feldman) are formal, expressivist and instrumentalist.*
4. *Art critics can be divided into two broad categories: conservative and radical critics.*

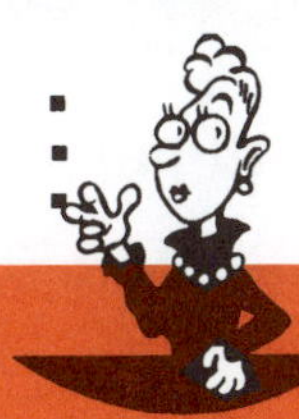

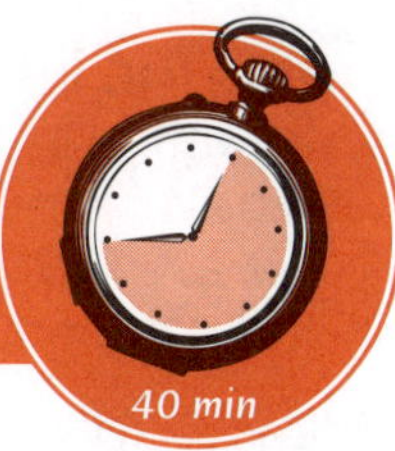

YOUR TOPIC INFO

What is the Role of the Art Historian?

1 **Art historians** map out the significance of artworks and artists in relation to their **contexts**: that is, the **periods of time** and the **places** in which they worked. Historians are interested in tracing how artists and artworks **gain status** and how **audiences relate to the artworks**. The practice of art history is very much a **puzzle-solving exercise** in which pieces are put together to provide a deeper insight into the connections between the **artwork**, the **artist** and the **audience**.

2 All historians seek to discover **meaning about artefacts** through researching and being familiar with the past. In many ways, artworks become **historical artefacts** when they are completed because they represent a particular **period of time** and reflect the **world** in which they are completed. For example, by looking at Rembrandt van Rijn's different styles and depictions of subject matter (himself) over time, an art historian can see aspects of the artist's life, his thoughts and events in history.

3 **Good art historians** will:

- suggest links between the **events of the time** and the way **society** and **individuals** thought and acted
- provide accounts of how **artists, styles and artworks** evolved
- evaluate the significance of **cultural qualities** (social, political, religious and gender aspects) in shaping artworks
- explain to contemporary audiences the **characteristic features** of artworks produced in previous eras
- situate **ideas and styles** in particular places and times.

Approaches to Art History

4 Accounts of history can be divided into two broad **categories**.

- **Historical narratives** give an account of the **events of the time**. They focus on 'What happened?' within the artworld.
- **Historical analysis** evaluates and deduces the **causes of actions and events** within a particular period in history. It focuses on the question of 'Why did it happen?'

It is the **interaction** of these two approaches that gives historical investigation its value in the study of the visual arts.

Studying Art History

5 Artworks should be considered as **primary sources** that provide a distinction between the **present and the past**. The artwork in a historical sense offers a 'window' into the past. Knowledge of the history of art can therefore assist you in assessing and analysing the **significance of artworks** and the **intentions of artists**.

6 If you were to compare the painting *The Three Graces* by Raphael with Picasso's *Les Demoiselles d'Avignon*, for example, you would be keenly aware of the **difference in style** and in the depiction of the female form. Both are figurative paintings, but their **different conventions and styles** will relate to the **different time periods** in which they were produced.

- A knowledge of **Renaissance art** would assist you in identifying the painting by Raphael. You could then discuss the conventions in the painting, such as ideas about absolute beauty, allegories, visual realism and humanism.
- In contrast to this painting is Picasso's **modernist depiction** of the female. To analyse this painting, you would need a knowledge of the transition of historic painting into modernism. You could outline the aims of the avant-garde in modernism, and reflect upon the grotesque female forms as the personal feelings of the artist in a society that was experiencing rapid social and political change.

7 There is a relationship between **art criticism** and **art history** that provides the basis for the evaluation of artworks and will assist you to make meaningful interpretations of art.

Art History in the HSC written Examination

8 A good knowledge of the historical details of your selected **case studies** ensures better preparation for the examination. It is important to make a link between the **historical periods** and the **artists** you have studied.

9 When writing about the history of art it is important that you understand and appreciate the **uniqueness of each time period** you are studying. Historical studies highlight how approaches to artmaking have varied greatly in different times.

10 When you are writing about history, you cannot simply judge or assess artworks using the conventions of artmaking today. You need to put your judgements into the **context of the historical time** so the examiner can see your understanding of history.

The Practice of Art History

11 The following mindmap shows a summary of different aspects of the **practice of art history**.

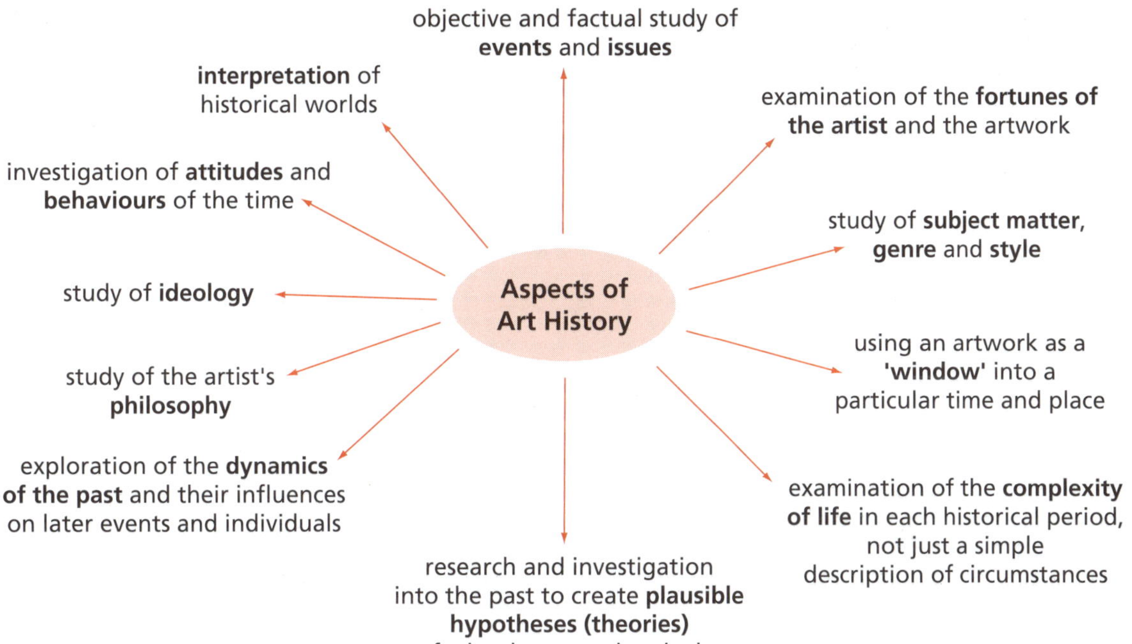

CHECKPOINT:

1. *Art historians study the significance of artworks and artists in relation to the periods of time and the places in which they worked.*
2. *The two broad types of art history are historical narratives and historical analyses.*
3. *Art history can help you to analyse and understand the significance of artworks and to get an idea of what an artist intended.*

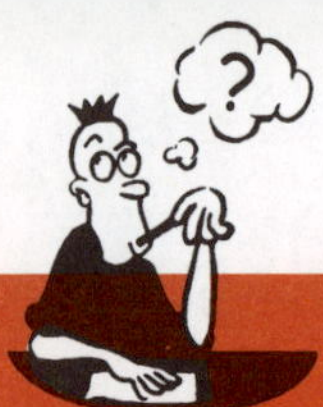

PRACTICE IN ARTMAKING, ART CRITICISM & ART HISTORY

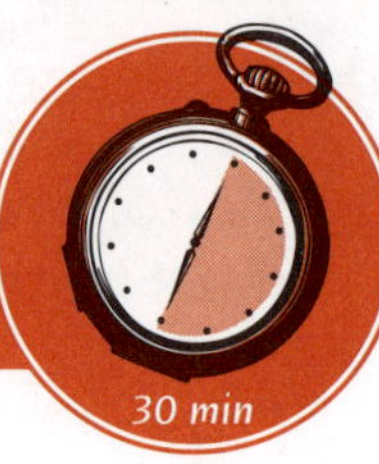

TEST YOUR KNOWLEDGE

1. What are the three key areas of practice within visual arts?

2. What is the purpose of studying the practice of artists, historians and critics in the visual arts?

3. What are some important issues in artmaking?

4. What is the purpose of art criticism?

5. Name three things a good art critic should do.

6. What is the purpose of art history?

7. Name four aspects of art history which an art historian should examine.

8. How important is interpretation and judgement to art criticism and art history?

☞ *Answers on pages 81–82*

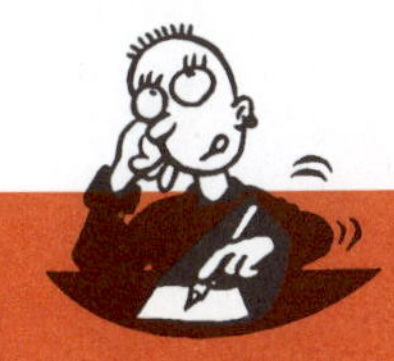

PRACTICE IN ARTMAKING, ART CRITICISM & ART HISTORY

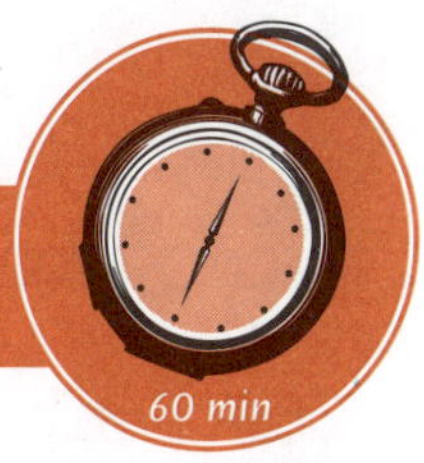

KEY EXAM QUESTIONS

These are the type of questions you will find in the HSC written Examination paper. They are divided into Section I with three compulsory questions and Section II in which one question out of six must be answered.
Note that there are many questions provided here which only cover the Practice component. This is not a sample exam paper—your exam will cover all of the content. See pages 74–79 for the Sample HSC Examination Paper.
To complete this section, you might choose one question from each section to answer (a total of four questions) and do them under exam-style conditions (90 minutes), or you might choose more questions and simply map out your answers in point form. Remember, though, that writing full exam-style answers is invaluable for practice.

Section I: Question 1 (5 marks each)

Please note that the value of Questions 1, 2 and 3 may vary from year to year but will always give a total mark of 25 for Section I.

Plate 1: Jean-Auguste-Dominique Ingres, *La Grand Odalisque*, 1814
Oil on canvas, 91 cm x 162 cm
Found in: Margaret Marsh et al, *ART: Art, Research and Theory*, Oxford University Press, Melbourne, 1999
www.artchive.com/artchive/I/ingres/ingres_grand_odalisque.jpg.html

Artmaking

1. Discuss the intentions of the artist in Plate 1.
2. Account for the approaches in artmaking in Plate 1.

Art Criticism

3. Critically assess Plate 1.
4. Account for key ideas found in Plate 1.

Art History

5. How does Plate 1 offer a 'window' into the past?
6. Looking at Plate 1, discuss the historical significance of the artwork.

Section I: Question 2 (8 marks each)

Plate 2: Anne Zahalka, *The Bathers*, 1989
Type C print, 90 cm x 74 cm
Found at: www.artgallery.nsw.gov.au/collection/works/96.1990/

☞ *Answers on pages 86–87*

Plate 3: Charles Meere, *Australian Beach Pattern,* 1940
Oil on canvas, 90.1 cm x 120.7 cm
Found in: Donald Williams, *Art Now: Contemporary Art Post-1970,* McGraw-Hill, Sydney, 1996

Plate 4: Yasumasa Morimura, *Blinded by the Light*, 1991
Colour photograph, 200 x 386 cm
Found in: Marsh, *ART: Art, Research and Theory*, 1999
www.artnet.com/artists/yasumasa-morimura/blinded-by-the-light-dvp0xCupyowa9-xLkPUePw2

Artmaking

7 Look at Plates 2 and 3. Give an account of the importance of materials in the development of each artist's approach to artmaking.

8 Discuss the influence of the audience and world on the artist's approach to artmaking. Refer to Plates 2, 3 and 4 in your response.

Art Criticism

9 Explain how art criticism provides better understanding of artworks. You must refer to Plates 2, 3 and 4 in your answer.

10 Look at Plates 2, 3 and 4. Give an account of how ideas about artmaking change over time.

Art History

11 Look at Plates 2, 3 and 4. Discuss how approaches to artworks change and vary over time.

12 How have ideas about representation been conveyed in art through history? You must make reference to Plates 2, 3 and 4.

Section I: Question 3

(12 marks each)

Plate 5: Colin McCahon, *Am I Scared,* 1976
Acrylics on paper, 730 x 1104 mm

Plate 6: Colin McCahon, *Storm Warning*, 1980–81
Acrylics on unstreached canvas, 1945 x 1810 mm

Plate 7: Colin McCahon, *Victory Over Death 2*, 1970
Synthetic polymer on canvas, 207.5 x 597.7 cm

All found in: Marsh, *ART: Art, Research and Theory*, 1999

☞ *Answers on pages 87–88*

Artmaking

13 Critically analyse this artist's use of materials and his intentions in artmaking. In your response make reference to Plates 5, 6 and 7.

Art Criticism

14 Using Plates 5, 6 and 7, analyse how the artist is responding to his world. Make reference to possible meanings that can be associated with the artworks.

Art History

15 Using Plates 5, 6 and 7, examine what significant events may have influenced the artist and how these are represented in his artworks.

Section II Questions (25 marks each)

Artmaking

16 Explore the importance of issues and ideas to artists' approaches to art. Provide examples to support your response.

17 Discuss how artists have interpreted their experiences through their artworks. Make reference to two or more artists you have studied.

Art Criticism

18 'Art critics provide the audience with a richer understanding of the artist's work.' Evaluate this statement and discuss the importance of the critic in visual arts. Support your response by making reference to artists and critics you have studied.

19 Explain how critics construct meaning in an artwork. Provide examples that support your explanation in your response.

Art History

20 Discuss how historical studies have provided a better understanding of the practice of visual arts. In your response, provide examples of artworks you have studied to support your answer.

21 'It is impossible to relive the past.' Evaluate this statement in terms of the historical value of artists and artworks you have studied.

☞ *Answers on pages 88–90*

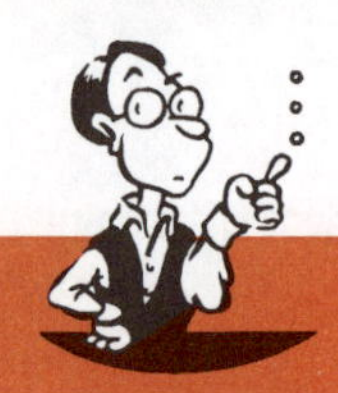

THE CONCEPTUAL FRAMEWORK
The Four Agencies in the Artworld

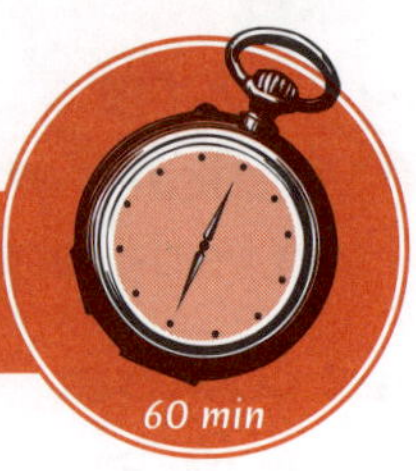

YOUR TOPIC INFO

What are the Four Agencies?

1 The **artworld** is a diverse and difficult area to study and fully comprehend. To make it easier to discuss and examine, the HSC Visual Arts syllabus has broken down the artworld into **four smaller components** known as **'agencies' in the artworld**. They are:

- Artist
- Artwork
- World
- Audience.

2 Each of these components helps highlights the **'cause and effect'** nature of the artworld. Art doesn't exist within a **social vacuum**. The Conceptual Framework demonstrates how **reliant** each agent is on the others in order to survive in the artworld.

3 This part of the course provides accounts and explanations of the **roles and relationships** of the four agencies which change radically over time. These roles and relationships change due to factors such as the **values and beliefs** of society, new uses of **technology, personal discoveries** of the artist and the **audiences' reception** of artworks.

How is the Conceptual Framework Useful?

4 The Australian art academic and writer **Joanna Mendelssohn** suggests that being critical about art is similar to pulling a clock apart, learning how it works and then putting it back together. This is exactly what the Conceptual Framework offers us—a way of understanding how **key agents** within the artworld function and interact with each other.

- The Conceptual Framework seeks to outline the **'who, what, when and why'** of the artworld by identifying **influencing factors**. It examines the **causes and effects** of events in the artworld.
- Understanding the Conceptual Framework provides a richer depth of knowledge about the **operation of the artworld** and the **relationships** that exist within it. The knowledge you will gain goes beyond the learning of dates and artistic movements to an understanding of **how art is created and received**.

- It highlights what **factors** contribute to the development of artists, styles, events and artworks.
- It can be easily used in the study of **art history** as much as it can be used to understand **contemporary art events**.

5 Unfortunately there are not too many books that will draw up a diagram for you which will link the Conceptual Framework to an art movement or event, but with a little knowledge about the **four agencies** (described on the next few pages) it will not be too difficult for you to develop your understanding of the Conceptual Framework.

The Artist

6 The **'artist'** is an identity attributed to one who **makes artworks**, establishes **modes of representation** (styles and genres) and ensures a **coherency of intention**. Artists attempt to make a connection with the audience through their artworks. The term 'artist' can apply to either an individual or a group involved in a **specific approach to artmaking**.

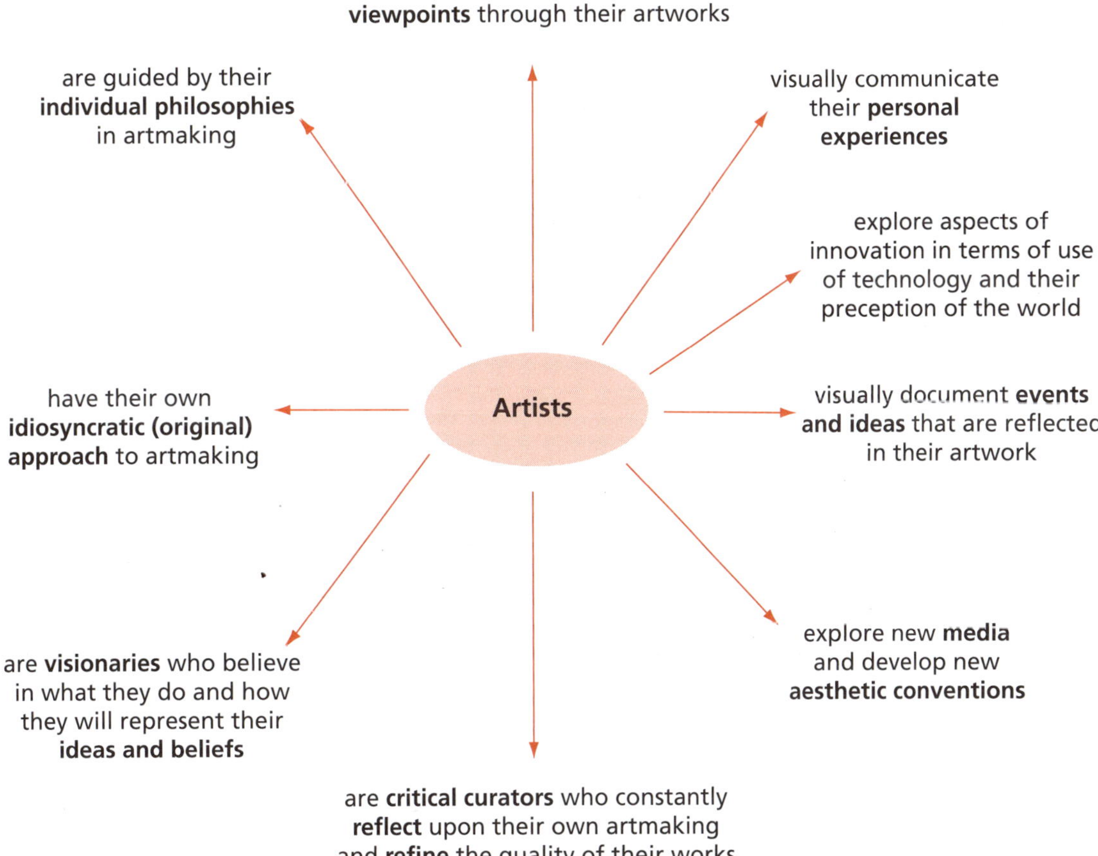

The Artwork

7 The **function of an artwork** has two aspects:

- The artwork is the object that demonstrates the **artist's intention** and communicates the **artist's ideas**.
- It can also be an artefact which shows the **permanency of the material**. This is done through the artist's own **technical innovation and finesse**.

8 The artwork is the **bridge** between the **audience** and the **artist**. Along this bridge there are endless possibilities for **interpreting** the artwork. The artwork can also be seen as a **product of the time and world** in which it was produced.

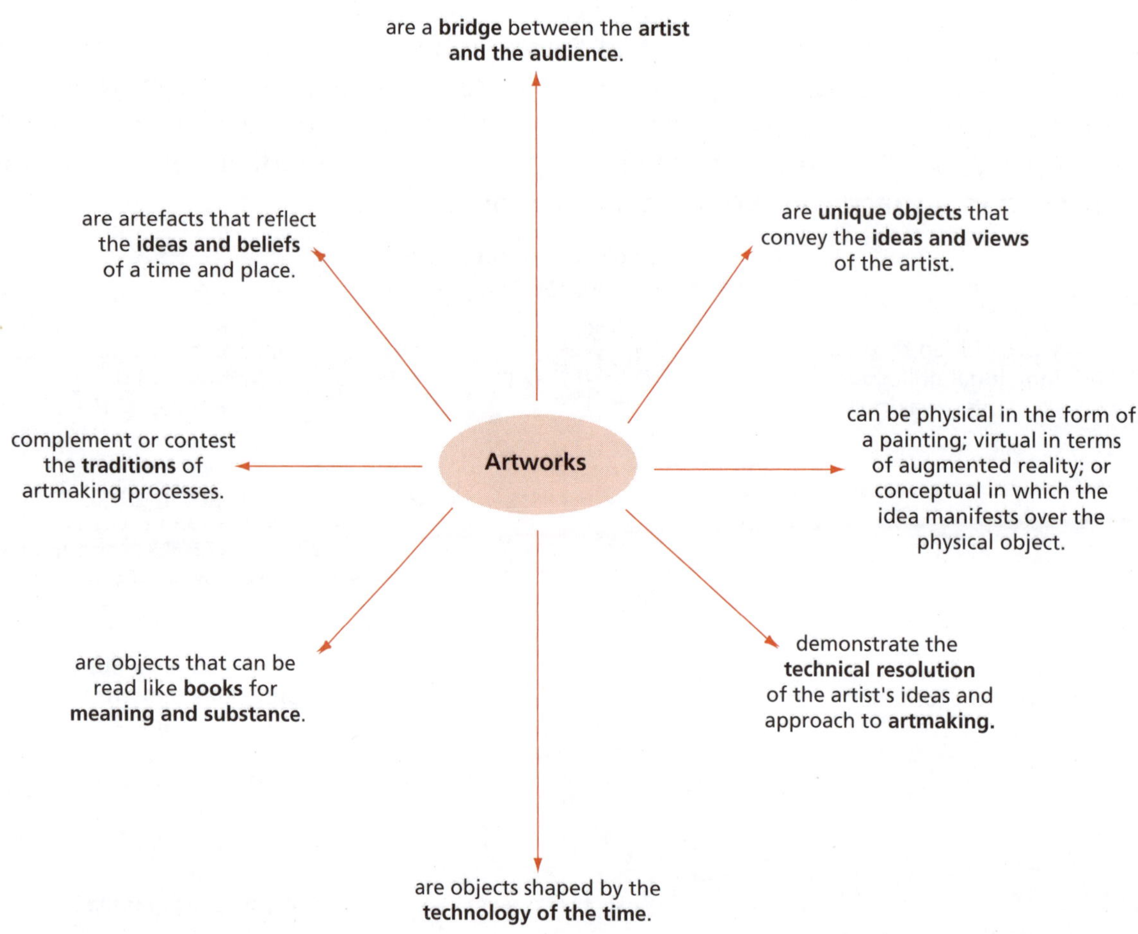

The World

9 This refers to the **time and place** in which the artist, artwork and audience resides. The important thing to remember is that the world also includes the **ideas** that are carried in particular times. Knowing about these ideas and beliefs will allow you to see the influences of history, modernism and postmodernism in artworks. **Events, individuals and the environment** have a significant impact on the artworld and it is important that you understand these in your study of visual arts.

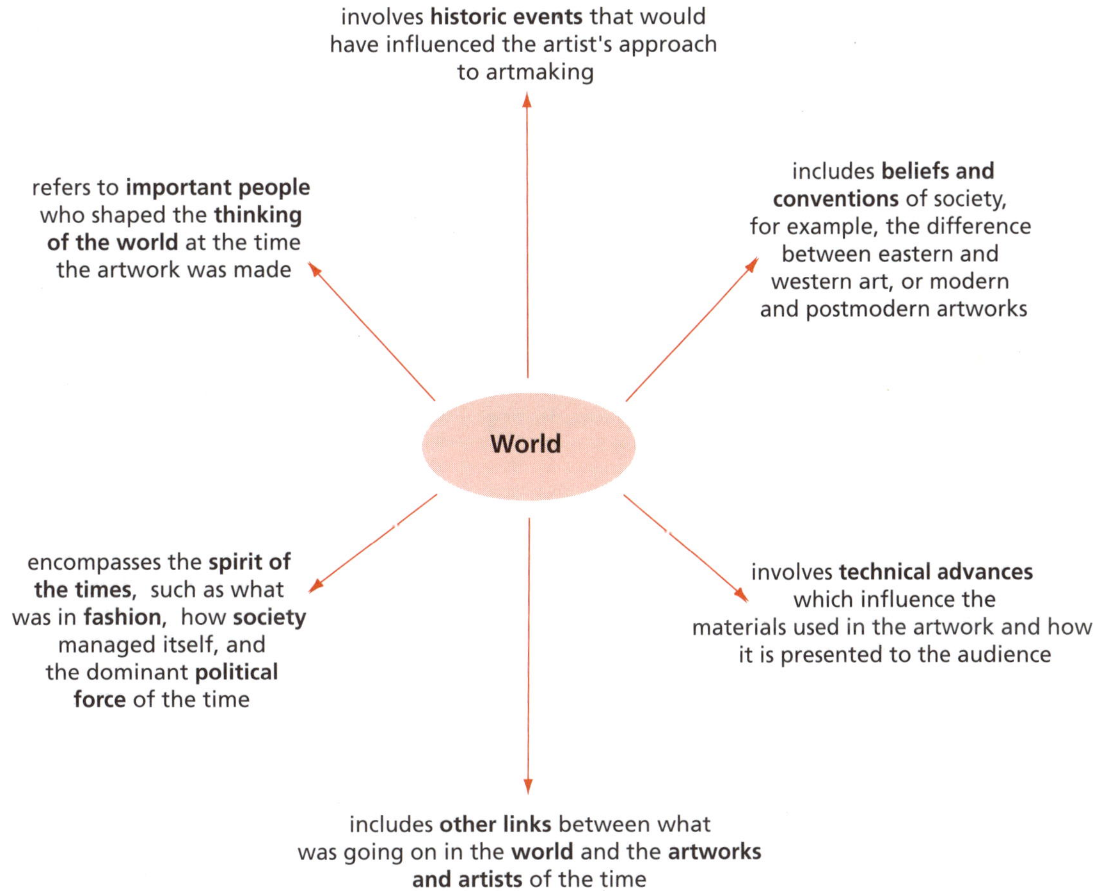

The Audience

10 The audience is made up of the people who **view and comment** upon artworks. Throughout history they have included **historians and critics** whose accounts of artists and artworks **document** the **thoughts and tastes** of the times. In the modern period particularly they were key individuals who offered **names and explanations** for new styles and approaches to artmaking.

11 Today, the audience constitutes **anyone who views artworks**, but the key agents are the **curators, critics, historians and art writers** who provide publicly accountable insights into artworks and artists. It is the audience which **contextualises** the information about the artworks through **critical and historical discussion**. The audience gives **value** to the artwork by clarifying its **intention and meaning**.

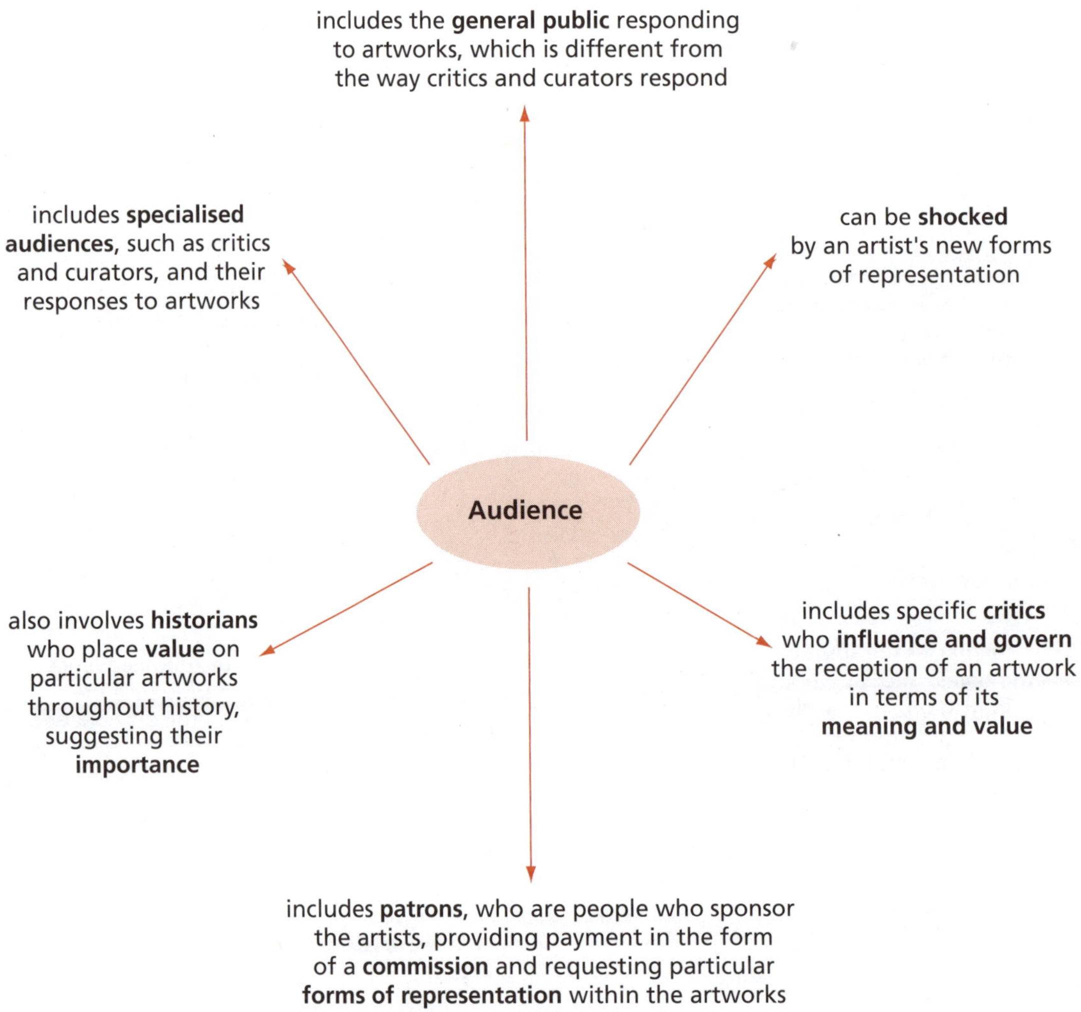

CHECKPOINT:

1. *The Conceptual Framework provides you with a way of understanding the relationships that exist within the artworld.*
2. *The four 'agencies' in the artworld which you study are the **artist**, the **artwork**, the **world** and the **audience**.*
3. *The Conceptual Framework emphasises that artworks are not produced in a social vacuum, but that the artist is affected by the world and the audience of the time.*

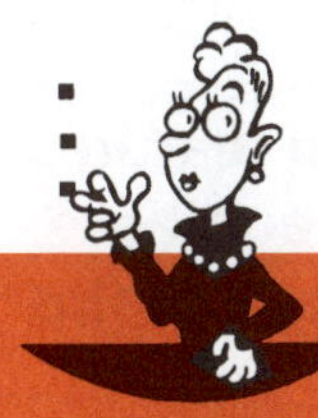

YOUR TOPIC INFO

Analysis Through the Conceptual Framework

1. The difficulty of using the Conceptual Framework is that there very few books about artworks or art movements which make specific reference to all **four agencies** at once. It is up to you to assemble all the information you have learned about the four agencies and use it to **analyse** parts of the artworld.
2. Below is an example of how to use the Conceptual Framework to analyse an **art movement**—in this case, **Pop art**. The outline demonstrates how the four agencies are **interrelated** and how they can be used for **evaluation and discussion**.

Pop Art: Conceptual Framework

Artist	Examples of artists in the Pop art movement: • Andy Warhol • Roy Lichtenstein • Robert Rauschenberg • Richard Hamilton • Jasper Johns • James Rosenquist • Claes Oldenberg
Artworks	• Warhol, *Marilyn Monroe Diptych,* 1962, screen-print on canvas • Lichtenstein, *Drowning Girl,* 1963, oil and synthetitc polymer on canvas • Rauschenberg, *Retroactive 1,* 1964, screen-print • Hamilton, *Just What Is It That Makes Today's Homes So Different, So Appealing?,* 1956, collage • Johns, *White Flag,* 1955, encaustic and collage on canvas • Rosenquist, *F-111,* 1965, oil on canvas and aluminium • Oldenberg, *Two Cheeseburgers, With Everything,* 1962, enamel painted over plaster
Audience	• Leo Castelli: curator who collected pop artists' work from the beginning of the movement • Max Kozloff: critic who investigated the development of pop art • Lawrence Alloway: English critic who first coined the term 'pop art' in 1959 • Robert and Ethel Scull: collectors of pop artists' works who championed their approach to artmaking
World	• Late 1950s and 1960s • The beat generation is developing into the hippie generation. • Television is invented. • The Cold War (political and military tension) between the USA and Soviet Union is at its height. • The Vietnam War sees the catastrophic involvement of the USA and Australia. • Bob Dylan is writing poetry and music that inspire the times. • Marilyn Monroe dies of a drug overdose. • John F Kennedy and Martin Luther King are assassinated. • The USA becomes the industrial capital of the democratic world. • Photographic screenprinting is extensively used in the fine arts and commercial world. • Student riots in Paris in 1968 highlight the questioning of authority in society.

This table of artists and events involved in pop art highlights the **main features** of pop art in each of the four agencies: artists, artworks, world and audience. The information can then be used to outline, in **more detail**, the relationships that were established in the development of Pop art.

3 Below is a diagram which demonstrates this. It illustrates the development of Andy Warhol's art using the four agencies. This time, however, it emphasises the **interaction** of the four agencies, rather than listing their features. This way we can see the **influences** of the world and the audience on Andy Warhol and his artwork.

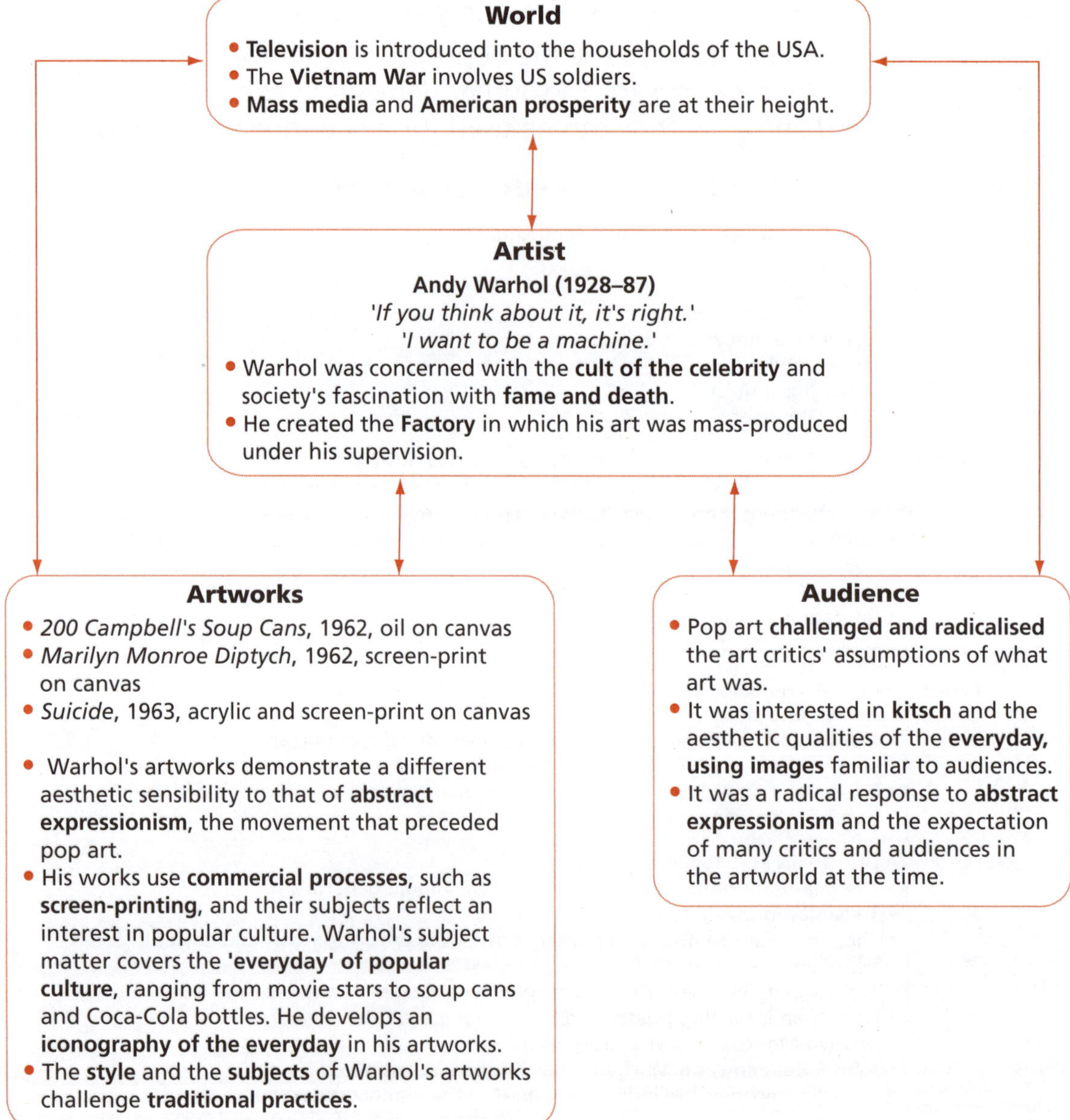

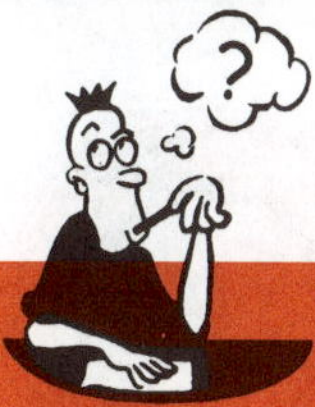

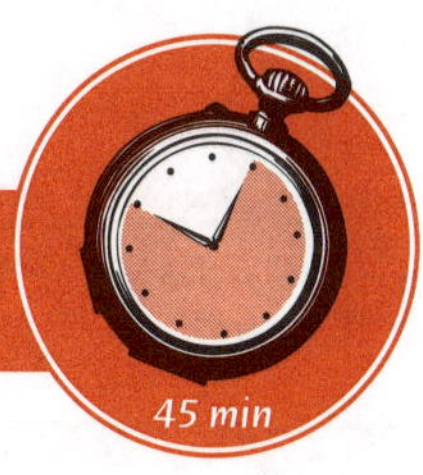

THE CONCEPTUAL FRAMEWORK

TEST YOUR KNOWLEDGE

1. What is the main aim of the Conceptual Framework?
2. Name the four agencies in the artworld and write a brief explanation of each one in point form.
3. What are three types of individuals that can be considered the 'audience' of artworks?
4. In the table below, write the key aspects of a case study, theme or art movement you have studied.

Artist(s)	
Artworks	
Audience	
World	

5. Using a diagram (in the same format as on page 38), fill in information about a particular artist you have studied and show how the artist and the artworks are affected by the world and the audience of the time.

☞ *Answers on pages 82–83*

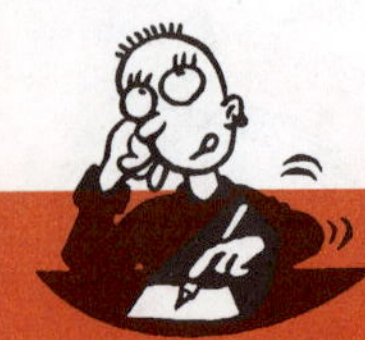

THE CONCEPTUAL FRAMEWORK

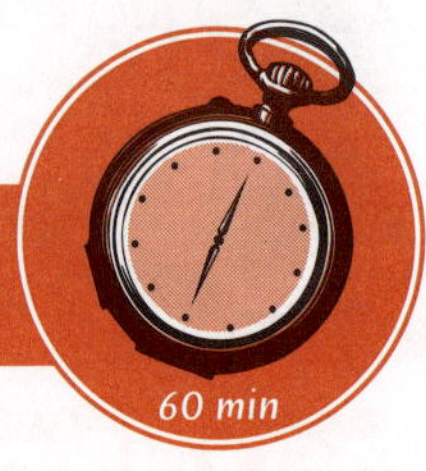

KEY EXAM QUESTIONS

See note about Key Exam Questions on page 29. Remember that the mark value for questions in Section I can vary.

Section I: Question 1 (4 marks each)

Plate 1: Leonardo Da Vinci, *The Last Supper*, 1497
Mural, 420 cm x 910 cm
Found in: Glenis Israel, *Artwise: Visual Arts 7–10*, Jacaranda Press, Milton, 1997
www.artchive.com/artchive/L/leonardo/lastsupp.jpg.html

1. Explain how the influences of the world can be seen in Plate 1.
2. Who is the intended audience for Plate 1? Why?

Section I: Question 2 (8 marks each)

Plate 2: Otto Dix, *Card Playing Cripple*, 1920
Oil on canvas, 105 cm x 86.5 cm
Found in: Robert Hughes, *The Shock of the New: Art and the Century of Change*, BBC, London, 1980

Plate 3: Barbara Kruger, *Untitled (Your Body is a Battleground)*, 1989
Photographic silkscreen on vinyl, 280 cm x 280 cm
Found in: Marsh, *ART: Art, Research and Theory*, 1999
www.thebroad.org/art/barbara-kruger/untitled-your-body-battleground

3. Describe the relationship between the audience and artist as seen in Plates 2 and 3.
4. Give an account of how the artists respond to the world in Plates 2 and 3.

Section I: Question 3 (13 marks each)

Plate 4: Andy Warhol, *200 Campbell's Soup Cans*, 1962
Oil on canvas, 180 cm x 250 cm
Found in: Hughes, *The Shock of the New*, 1980
www.moma.org/learn/moma_learning/andy-warhol-campbells-soup-cans-1962/

☞ *Answers on pages 90–91*

Plate 5: Andy Warhol , *Suicide (Purple Jumping Man)*, 1963
Acrylic and silk screen enamel on canvas, 205 cm x 205 cm
Found in: Hughes, *The Shock of the New,* 1980
www.artimage.org.uk/8499/andy-warhol/suicide--purple-jumping-man---1963

Plate 6: Andy Warhol, *Marilyn Diptych*, 1962
Acrylic and silkscreen on canvas, 208 cm x 145 cm
Found in: Hughes, *The Shock of the New,* 1980
www.painsley.org.uk/gallery/p2a7b.htm

Warhol celebrated the banality and excessiveness of popular culture. His art displayed an aesthetic that was generated from movies, newspapers and advertising and owed its heritage to Duchamp's 'readymades'. He stood for a new artistic order that saw the demise of the well-crafted 'art object'.

5. Look at Plates 4, 5 and 6 and the text extract, and evaluate the importance of the relationship between the audience and the artwork.

6. Analyse how the artist has explored his world through his artworks, referring to Plates 4, 5 and 6.

Section II Questions (25 marks each)

7. Select two or more artists you have studied and explain how they sought to change the world through their art.

8. 'Art has nothing to do with the physical world. It is purely a product of the imagination of the artists.' Do you agree? Discuss, giving reasons for your answer.

☞ *Answers on pages 91–92*

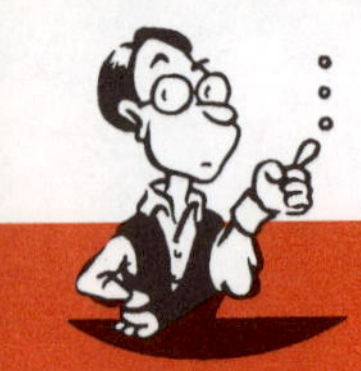

THE FRAMES
What are the Frames?

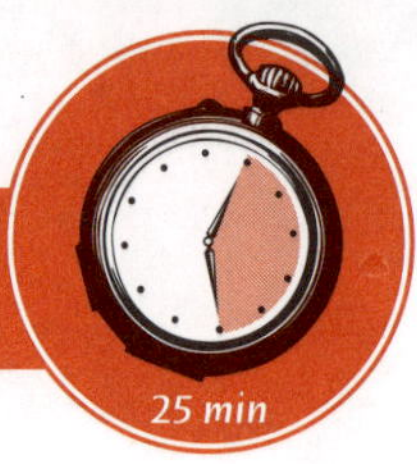

YOUR TOPIC INFO

The Four Frames

1. The Frames component of your HSC Visual Arts study shows you how to understand artworks and artists by looking at and analysing them through **particular structures**. These structures are known as the **Frames**, and they will give you 'keys' to opening up the **meanings** in artworks.

2. The Frames offer **four main ways** to study an artwork and analyse the intentions of the artist:
   - **Subjective**. This looks at the feelings and emotional responses we can get from artworks. It identifies the personal responses of artists and audiences.
   - **Structural**. This looks at the approach to form and the treatment of the materials in the artwork. It scrutinises how the artwork is put together and what technology is used.
   - **Cultural**. This deals with the way the artist and/or artwork develops a particular identity or characteristic that reflects the attitudes of a particular time or place.
   - **Postmodern**. This looks at artworks using contemporary knowledge and critical theories that were established in the 1980s to challenge traditional and modernist ideas.

How are the Frames Useful?

3. **Making sense of artworks**

These four Frames—subjective, structural, cultural and postmodern—provide **systems** for learning about artworks and **making sense** of them. Using the Frames to analyse artworks is like looking through four different telescopes which **focus** upon certain **details**. They provide a way for you to study unfamiliar artworks and find **meaning** in them.

4. **Deciphering codes**

You can also think of the Frames as a way of unlocking the complex **symbolic codes** found within artworks; that is, the 'language' of visual art. By being aware of the Frames, you are able to come to a more **sophisticated understanding** of artworks. The Frames enable you to recognise the complex and often puzzling organisation of an artwork.

5 **Putting artworks into their contexts**

The Frames can also help you to **contextualise artworks**, which means understanding them by looking at the kinds of places, times and structures they come from. They are the **supports** that allow us to unpack and examine the significant components of an artwork and its surrounding circumstances.

6 **Providing parameters for study**

The Frames establish intelligent **parameters** (boundaries, groupings) in which you can study an artwork. They offer us different **criteria** to use for investigating the **Conceptual Framework** (artworks, artists, audiences and the world) as well as the actions of critics and historians (**Practice**).

7 **Highlighting important aspects of artworks**

Using the Frames will enable you to see what is **significant in an artwork**, highlighting the most important elements within it.

The Frames in the HSC Written Examination

8 You will need to know how to appropriately **apply** the Frames and discuss their **significance** in the analysis of artworks. How you do this will depend on the question in the exam. It is worth spending some time reviewing their importance and how they can be applied to the **assessment of artworks** before the exam.

Each of the **four Frames**—subjective, structural, cultural and postmodern—is discussed separately on the following pages.

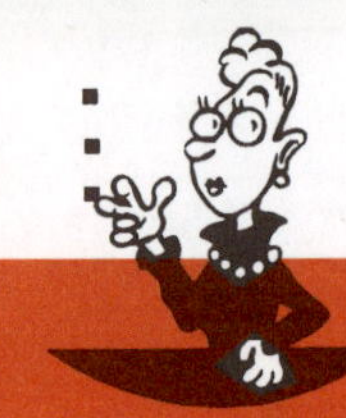

THE FRAMES
The Subjective and Structural Frames

YOUR TOPIC INFO

The Subjective Frame

1. Since the visual arts is an area in which personal and intimate qualities play vital roles, the Subjective Frame focuses on the **personal relationships** that both the artists and the audience have with an artwork and with writings about art. It looks at the way in which the audience will attempt to understand the **personal ideas** of the artist and the different ways people will **respond** to the artwork.

2. Using the Subjective Frame to look at an artwork (or a piece of art writing) involves asking **questions** such as:
   - How are **feelings and experiences** conveyed through the work?
   - What **personal understanding** of the subject is apparent and how is **communicated**?
   - Do you, as the audience, **feel and understand** the work?
   - What **personal insights** are offered by the artist/historian/critic?
   - Does the **title** of the work give a deeper insight to the work?
   - What **emotional responses** is the artist/historian/critic trying to get from the audience?
   - How is the **personality** of the artist/historian/critic conveyed?
   - How crucial is **imagination** to the production to an artwork, and why?
   - How are **individual styles** resolved in the artwork?
   - In what ways does the audience **empathise** with (identify with) the artist/historian/critic?
   - How are **personal intentions** conveyed through the artwork or writing?

3 Here is a mindmap showing **key aspects** of the Subjective Frame.

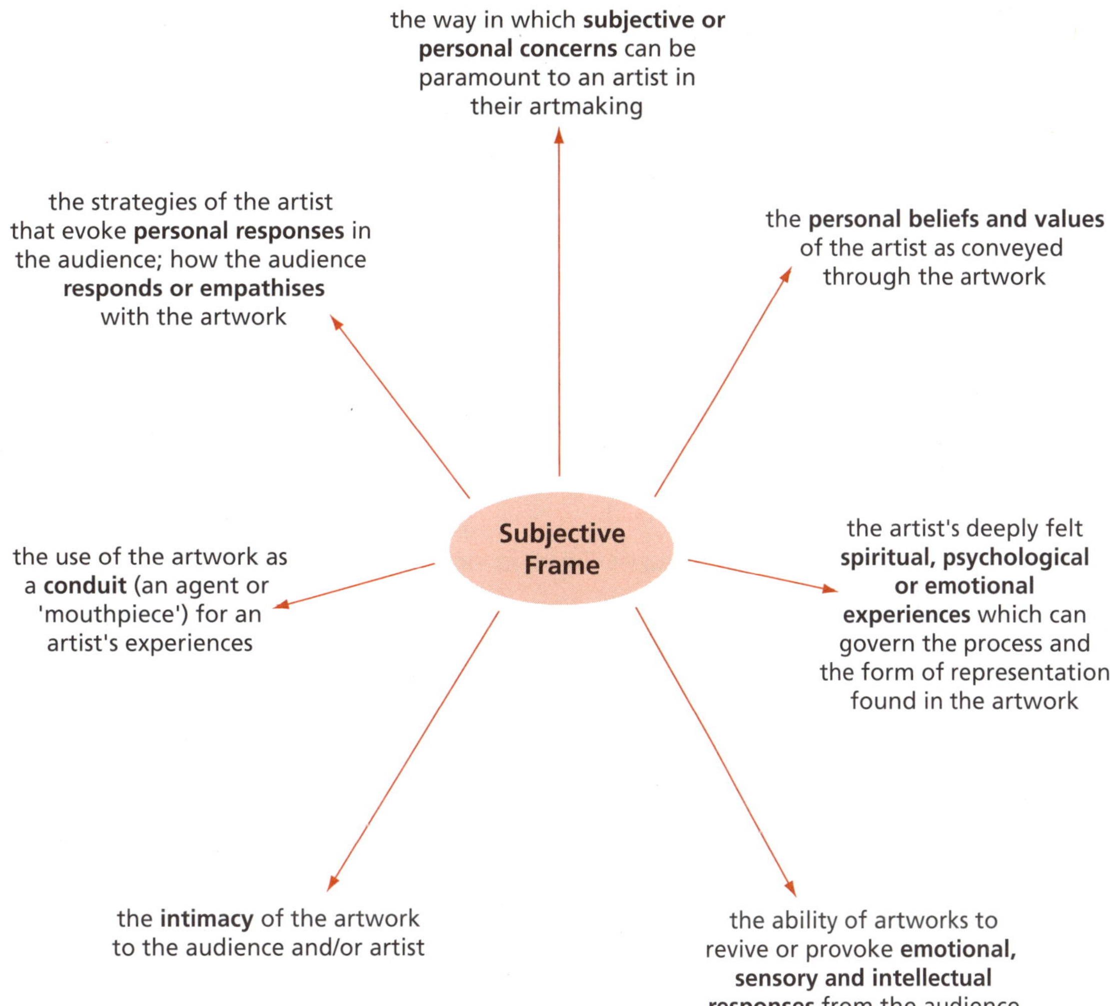

Structural Frame

4 Within the visual arts, **rules and conventions** have been established to guide and develop approaches to artmaking. Even the activity of **going against these standards** (as demonstrated by the avant-garde artists of the modernist period, for example) highlights in itself a **specific structure of artmaking** that ignores traditional conventions. Within each practice there are conventions that artists adhere to and which can be assessed in a formal manner. The **Structural Frame** provides an account of these rules and conventions in an artwork, and how the work is **pieced together**. It provides an understanding about the **form of the artwork** and reveals the **material and aesthetic qualities** that make the work unique.

5 The **Structural Frame**, therefore, seeks to explain:

- how artworks are **made**
- the artist's **intentions** in the artwork
- the types of **visual languages** used in artworks, and how these function
- how artworks use different **signs and symbols** and how these are **understood** by an audience.

6 **Art historians and critics** use the Structural Frame to study the **symbols and signs** in an artwork. Through this they can understand how **ideas and concepts** are conveyed, and how they may relate to particular stylistic rules or conventions found in different historical periods.

7 Using the **Structural Frame** to look at an artwork involves asking **questions** such as:

- Does the artwork suggest the use of **organisation** to compose the artwork? How?
- What **aesthetic principles** does the artist employ in the production of the artwork?
- What **symbols and codes** are used by the artist to convey ideas or experiences?
- How is the artwork **composed** and what are some of the **unique qualities** attributed to it?
- Is there a **system** to the way the artist/historian/critic conveys the message?
- What is particular about the **arrangement of the artwork** and how important is **order and placement**?

- What **visual conventions** are important to the artist?
- **Communicative value** refers to how well an artist, historian or critic can **express their ideas** through the use of **codes and conventions**. How has the artwork or art writing communicated its ideas through these conventions?

8 Below is a mindmap of the **issues** involved in using the Structural Frame.

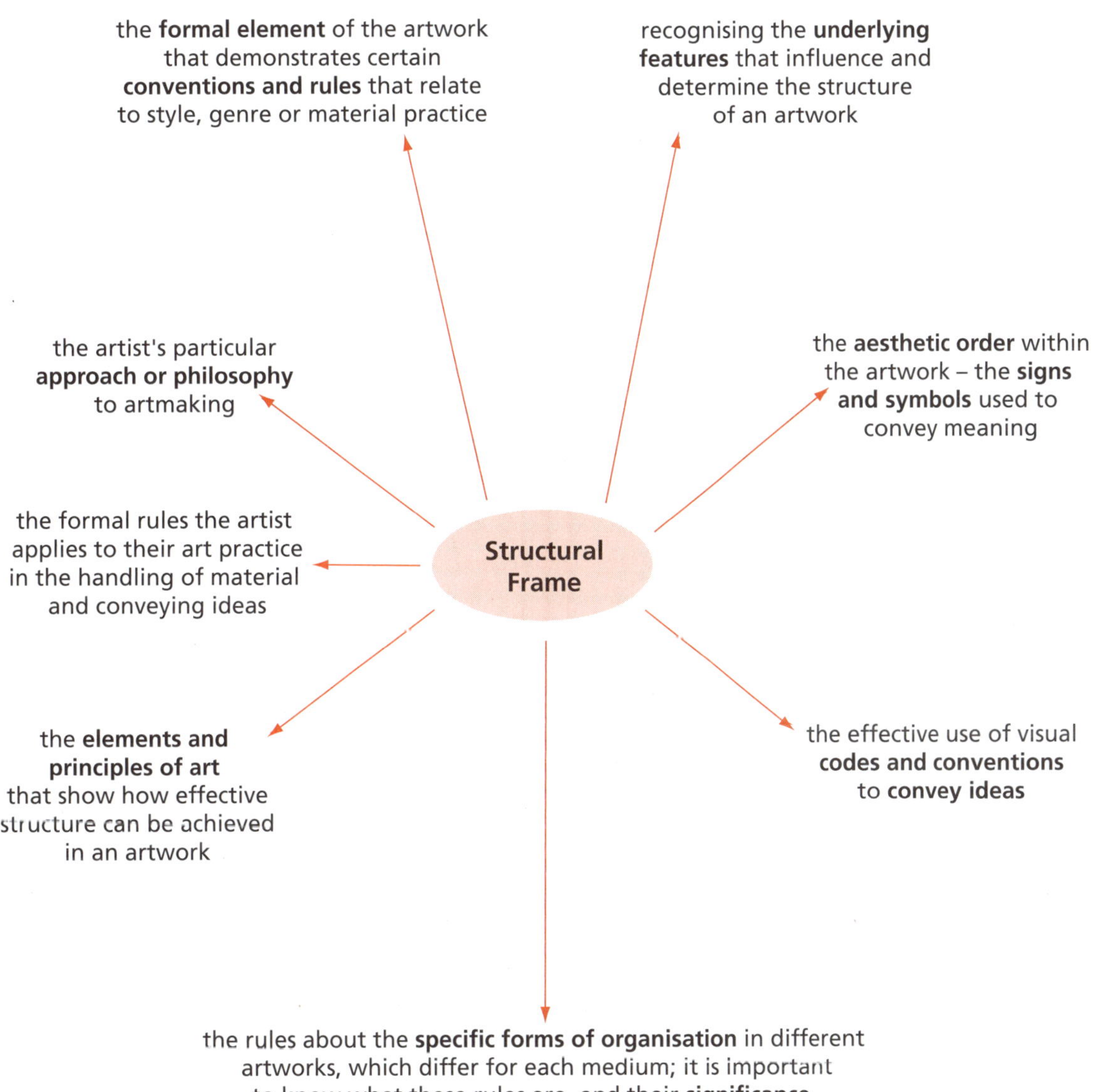

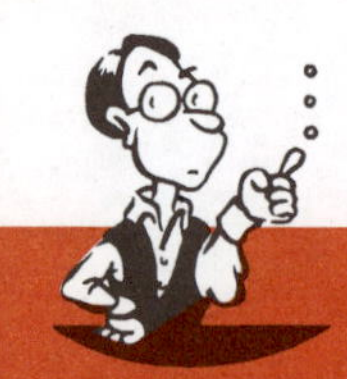

THE FRAMES

The Cultural and Postmodern Frames

YOUR TOPIC INFO

Cultural Frame

1. The **Cultural Frame** highlights the fact that no artist works in a **social vacuum** and that all artworks reflect **some aspects of the culture** (the beliefs, ideas and social structures) in which they were produced. For example, the **culture** which produced Aboriginal rock carvings in central Australia is vastly different to that which produced academic paintings in eighteenth century France. This demonstrates how the **time and place** will greatly influence both the **cultural significance** of the artwork and the **artist's approach to artmaking**. It is important that you make this distinction when learning about the Cultural Frame as it will help you understand the artwork and artist in terms of their **social identity and meaning**. The HSC Visual Arts syllabus also refers to the term **ideology**, which means the **values and beliefs** held by a society.

2. The Cultural Frame can be used, for example, in looking at the genre of **still life painting** throughout history:
   - The **Dutch painters of the 1800s** sought to represent the genre of still life in a **highly realistic manner**. They attached particular **symbolic qualities** to the works using the **visual conventions** of the time.
   - In contrast, the still life paintings of the **Cubists** reflected a **changed perception** of the subject matter and employed different **visual conventions** that reflected the values of the time—they sought to discover **new ways** of viewing the world, rather than the traditional, naturalistic ways of the earlier painters.

3. It is the Cultural Frame which alerts the audience to the **artist's philosophy and intention** by looking at the **culture** which surrounds the artwork. This also applies to **art historians and critics** who must take into consideration the cultural expectations and influences on artists and artworks.

4. Using the Cultural Frame to look at an artwork involves asking **questions** such as:
   - Are the **signs and symbols** used by the artist **specific to a particular culture**? How might other cultures understand this?

- Does the artist attempt to reflect the **attitudes of a time and place**? How is this done?
- Beliefs about **race, gender and social class** can shape a society. These elements can be **distilled** in an artwork, giving an insight into the cultural values of the artist's world. How are these conveyed in the artwork?
- What **ideological values** are represented in the artwork?
- Is there a **political significance** in the artwork? What is it? Why is it there?
- Are there obvious **political issues** in the writings of art critics and historians?

5 Below is a mindmap of the issues involved in using the **Cultural Frame**.

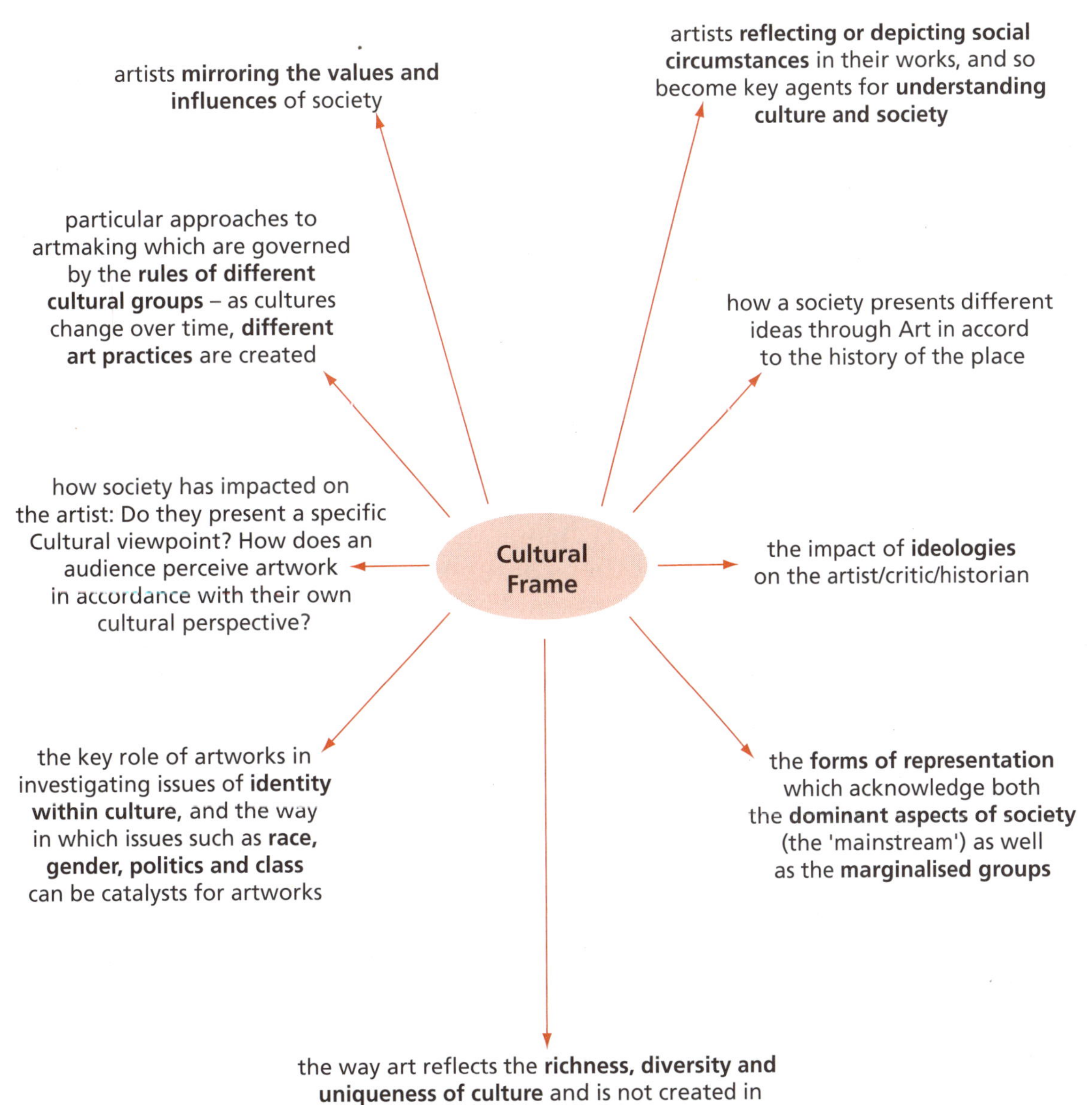

Postmodern Frame

6 The **Postmodern Frame** refers to the **critical debates** that are current in society and the artworld today. **Postmodernism** is a way of thinking which suggests that everything can be explained and interpreted in a number of **different ways** due to the changing nature of **what is true** and how we accept **facts**. This can be the most difficult frame to understand as it tends to escape clear definition, yet it is highly significant in the contemporary world.

7 In **postmodernism**:

- The idea of **absolute rules, dominant styles and recognised conventions**—as established in historic and modernist practices of criticism, history and artmaking—is dismissed.
- **Accepted conventions**—such as 'taste', 'culture' and 'style'—are critically brought into question and their validity is challenged.
- **Representation** is constructed by conditions between the artist, artwork and audience that can **change at any moment** and cannot be governed by **universal laws**.
- The **meaning and significance of art** can **evolve** (or devolve) at any given moment.
- There is a proposal that perhaps what is more important than the artwork is the **way we look and understand the work**, which even suggests that the **audience** is more important than the **artist**. Thus the role of the audience is crucial in interpreting the artwork.
- Approaches to artmaking such as **appropriation** (copying an object or image from another visual source), **irony** (using humour or satire as an aesthetic convention), **recontextualisation** (changing or shifting the perceived meaning of an image or object to another context) and **eclecticism** (a style of art in which features are borrowed from various other artistic styles) are not necessarily new, but they do challenge **traditional modes of thinking.** They highlight the constantly changing nature of art and the fluid quality of 'meaning'.

8 Whilst **modernism** presented the visual arts as a search for **objectivity** within the artist's practice, **postmodernity** suggests there can only be **subjectivity** within these practices, that is, there can be no objective judgement of the value of artworks.

9 Using the **Postmodern Frame** to look at an artwork involves asking **questions** such as:

- How do the artworks challenge the **authority of history**?
- Are traditions in art **disregarded** by the artist? How?
- What **conventions are being critiqued** (criticised) by the artist?

- How are **signs and symbols** being reinvented to create new meanings?
- Are conventions such as **parody, appropriation, irony and wit** used in the work?
- Does the artist **recontextualise** (put into a new context) the source of the image to create a different meaning?
- Have there been multiple **reinterpretations** of the artwork?
- Does the artwork seek to highlight the issues of **marginalised groups** in society?
- How does the artwork destabilise the **audience's expectations**?
- How do some artists show an **anti-authoritarian** approach in their artmaking?

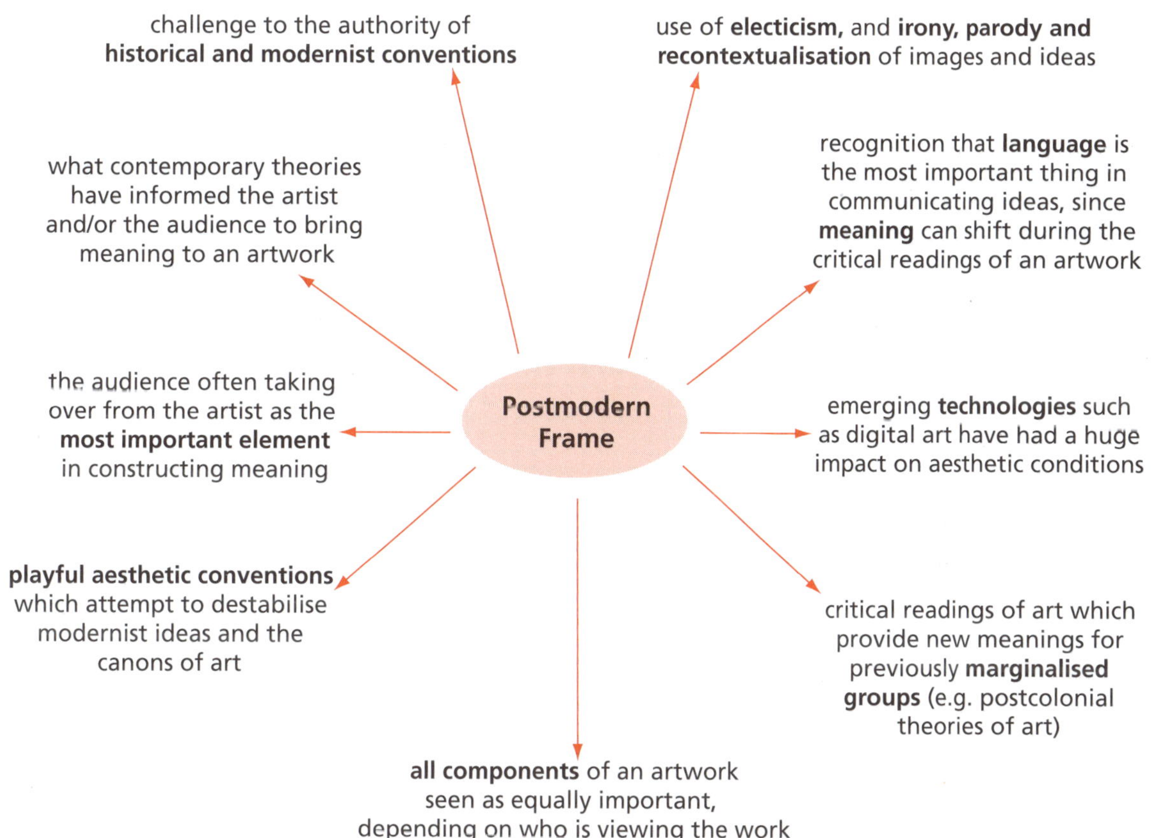

CHECKPOINT:

1. *The four Frames provide four focus areas for analysing artworks.*
2. *The Subjective Frame concentrates on the personal and emotional responses generated by an artwork, and the intentions of the artist.*
3. *The Structural Frame focuses on the rules and conventions followed in an artwork.*
4. *The Cultural Frame looks at the ideas and beliefs surrounding artiosts and artworks, which come from specific times and places in history.*
5. *The Postmodern Frame suggests there are many different meanings in artworks, and the audience who interprets them can be more important than the artist's intentions.*

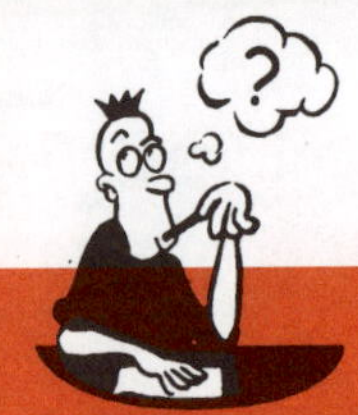

THE FRAMES

TEST YOUR KNOWLEDGE

1. Outline three key aspects of each of the four frames: subjective, structural, cultural and postmodern.

2. What personal or 'subjective' qualities can be associated with an artwork?

3. What are signs and symbols used in art? How are they used?

4. What is postmodernism?

5. How do cultural values influence the artist?

☞ *Answers on pages 84–85*

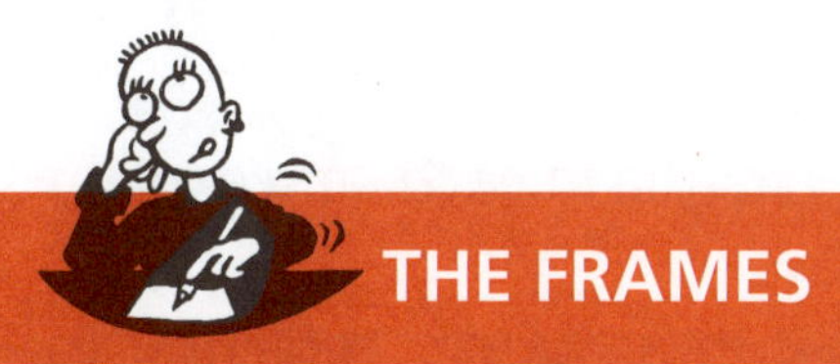

THE FRAMES

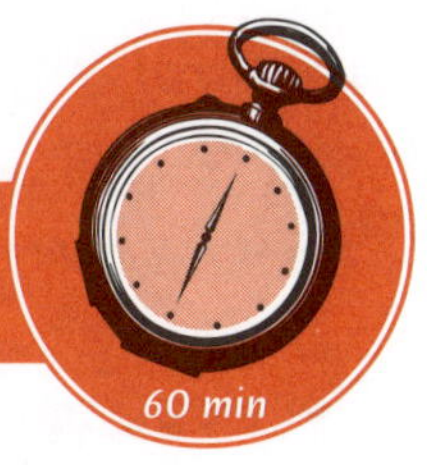

KEY EXAM QUESTIONS

See note about Key Exam Questions on page 29. Remember that the mark value for questions in Section I can vary.

Section I: Question 1

(5 marks each)

Plate 1: Gordon Bennett, *The Outsider*, 1988
Oil, synthetic polymer on canvas, 290 cm x 180 cm
Found in: Donald Williams and Colin Simpson,
Art Now: Contemporary Art Post-1970, McGraw-Hill, Sydney, 1996

Subjective

1. How important is the imagination of the artist in Plate 1?

Structural

2. Discuss the effectiveness of the visual structure of the artwork in Plate 1.

Cultural

3. How does Plate 1 construct a view of the society in which the artist lives?

Postmodern

4. How important is the technique of *appropriation* to Plate 1?

Section I: Question 2

(8 marks each)

Plate 2: Charles Meere, *Australian Beach Pattern,* 1940
Oil on canvas, 90.1 cm x 120.7 cm
Found in: Williams and Simpson, *Art Now*, McGraw-Hill, Sydney, 1996

Plate 3: Anne Zahalka, *The Bathers,* 1989
Type C print, 90 cm x 74 cm
Found in: Williams and Simpson, *Art Now*, McGraw-Hill, Sydney, 1994
www.artgallery.nsw.gov.au/collection/works/96.1990/

Subjective

5. Compare and contrast the different personal depictions of the same setting in Plates 2 and 3.

☞ *Answers on pages 92–93*

Structural

6. Look at Plates 2 and 3. Evaluate the different uses of media in each, and explain briefly how they are developed in the artworks.
7. Discuss how visual codes and conventions are used in artworks, referring to Plates 2 and 3 in your answer.

Cultural

8. What do the two works tell the audience about the treatment of race and gender in art?

Postmodern

9. *Irony* and *appropriation* are two key conventions within postmodern art. Discuss these in reference to Plates 2 and 3.

Section I: Question 3 (12 marks each)

Plate 4: Jean-Auguste-Dominique Ingres, *La Grand Odalisque*, 1814
Oil on canvas, 91 cm x 162 cm
Found in: Marsh, *ART: Art, Research and Theory*, 1999
www.wikiart.org/en/jean-auguste-dominique-ingres/the-grande-odalisque-1814

Plate 5: Willem De Kooning, *Woman III*, 1954
Oil on canvas.
Found in: Marsh, *ART: Art, Research and Theory*, 1999

Plate 6: Wendy Sharpe, Diana of Erskineville, 1996
Oil on canvas.
Found in: Marsh, *ART: Art, Research and Theory*, 1999
www.artgallery.nsw.gov.au/prizes/archibald/1996/19655/

The human figure has been a source of inspiration for artmaking throughout history, and its depiction has varied greatly. The changing representations of the human form demonstrate artists' changing perceptions and ideas about the body, which include the idealised form developed in Romanticism, the expressive concerns explored by modernist artists, and the development of conceptual concerns explored in postmodern art. Central to all these artists' intentions and actions is the depiction of humanity and physical presence.

Subjective

10. Investigate the significance of personal perception in the artist's approach to artmaking. Refer to Plates 4, 5 and 6 and the text in your answer.

☞ *Answers on pages 93–95*

Structural

11 Look at Plates 4, 5 and 6 and the text. Examine the way each artist constructs artworks, considering their formal qualities, style and intention.

Cultural

12 What significance has gender played upon the artists' approach to artmaking? Refer to Plates 4, 5 and 6 and the text in your answer.

Postmodern

13 Look at Plates 4, 5 and 6 and the text. How can the artworks be reinterpreted by a contemporary audience?

Section II Questions (25 marks each)

Subjective

14 Evaluate the importance of personal values and beliefs in artists you have studied. Give examples of artworks to support your response.

15 How has spirituality been an important source for artists you have studied? Give examples of artworks to support your response.

Structural

16 'Form or structure can be the most important element in an artwork.'
Discuss, referring to two or more artists you have studied.

17 'Artworks operate within specific codes and conventions that convey meaning.'
Do you agree? Refer to artworks that you have studied in your answer.

Cultural

18 How have artworks reflected the spirit of a time and place? Make specific reference to artworks you have studied.

19 Analyse how artists employ systems of signs and symbols to convey ideas about culture and society.

Postmodern

20 How has postmodern art sought to redefine the world?

21 How important is irony in art? Discuss, making reference to specific artworks you have studied.

☞ *Answers on pages 95–98*

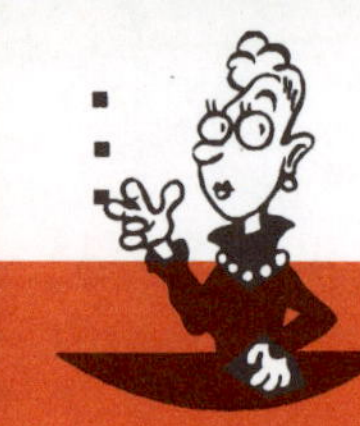

CASE STUDIES IN THE HSC
Using Case Studies

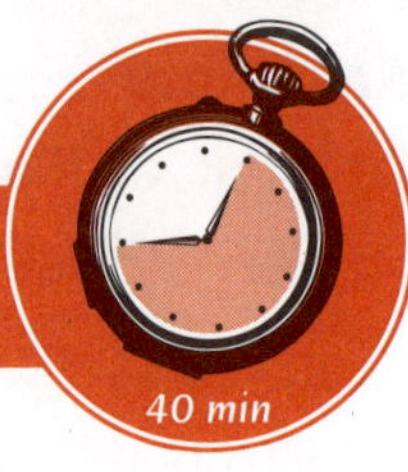

YOUR TOPIC INFO

This section gives some sample case studies and ideas for further case studies, but as part of your revision you will need to spend several hours revising the case studies you have studied in class. Make sure you can apply your knowledge of the content (Practice, Conceptual Framework and the Frames) to each of them. The tables on pages 64–65 can help you do this for each of your case studies.

What are Case Studies?

1. In the HSC Visual Arts course, you will look at a series of **case studies**. These are **in-depth studies of artists, artworks and art movements** which focus on particular **themes, issues or areas** in the visual arts. Case studies ensure that your knowledge of the HSC content is used with specific topics, and allow you to study art history and art criticism using real examples.

2. **Case studies** provide the opportunity for you to examine:
   - artistic **approaches**
   - artistic **intention**
   - use of **materials**
   - particular **processes** to make artworks
   - key issues concerning **forms of representation**.

3. Your study of the case studies will help you build up knowledge of **different forms of representation** found in art. **'Representation'** includes such aspects as styles, themes, genres, critical theories, historical narratives, use of technology and aesthetic conventions. Let's look more closely at some of these terms.

   Style: a recognisable manner in which an artwork is represented. Often it will be related to a 'school' of artmaking, or an art movement.

   Theme: the subject matter or ideas being communicated through the artwork.

   Critical theories: the development of postmodern ideas and concepts which pay close attention to development in art both historically and in the contemporary field. Art theory attempts to critique ways of understanding art.

   Historical narratives: These examine how artworks and artists inform their audiences about periods of time. They provide an insight into specific times and places and their influences on society and the artmaking of the period.

   Use of technology: Different technologies have emerged over time, and these offer many different ways of creating art and representing ideas. Consider for instance the differences between an oil painting and an audio-visual installation.

Selecting Case Studies

4 You must study a **minimum of five case studies** for your HSC. The selection of the case studies is up to your teacher. You will need them for both **Section I and Section II** of the HSC written Examination paper.

5 The selection for the case studies can **vary widely**. The important thing to assess is how **helpful** the case studies will be in preparing you to answer the questions in the HSC written Examination paper.

- If your case studies are **too broad** and your knowledge is **too general**, you run the risk of responding to exam questions in a much too prosaic (boring) manner.
- If, on the other hand, your case studies are **too narrow or specialised** (in topic area and/or the study of artists), you might find it difficult to select an appropriate question to answer in Section II of the paper (extended responses).

Planning your Case Studies

6 Case studies are the place where **raw information** about artists, designers, critics, historian and their works is **synthesised** (combined or merged) with the **content of the HSC Visual Arts course**—Practice, Conceptual Framework and the Frames.

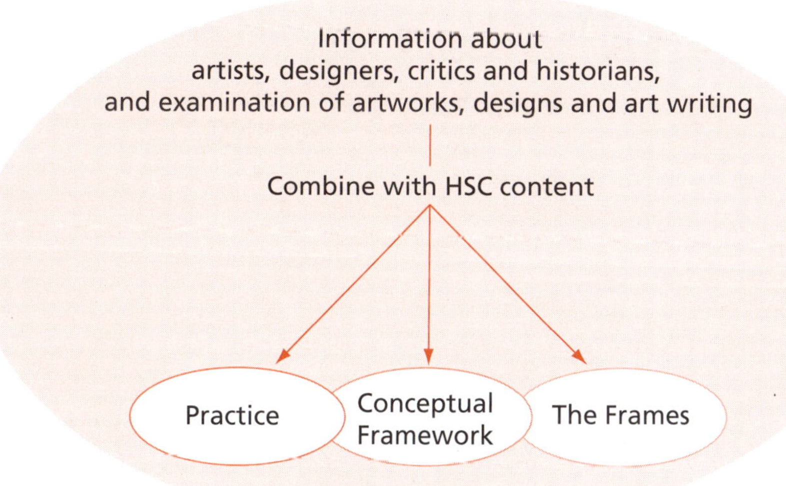

TIPS

- How can you **maximise your knowledge** of the visual arts through these case studies?
- How can you **structure your case studies** so you can strengthen your understanding and written expression in preparation for the examination?

- Identify the **weaknesses** in your knowledge of visual arts. How can these be strengthened by incorporating them into case studies?
- Are there any **exhibitions** you can visit that may be incorporated into one of your case studies?
- Do your case studies evenly apply the **Practice/Conceptual Framework/ Frames**, or do they concentrate more on one aspect according to the particular nature of the case study?
- Try to make the case studies reflect your **interests and strengths** in visual arts. Attempt to select artists who you are interested in and who may even assist you in your own artmaking.
- The first case study should be quite **simple**, but each case study that follows should become more complex.
- The case studies should **sharpen your investigative skills**. By the completion of the case studies you should have no trouble deciphering information and fitting it into the Practices/Conceptual Framework/Frames areas.
- Your case studies should be varied so that you familiarise yourself with the **broad range of representation** found in historical and contemporary art.

7 On the following pages is a list of **five sample case studies** which demonstrates the kind of artworks, key texts and videos that could be reviewed for each one. Please note that these are only **examples** of the organisation of case studies. You and your teacher may approach the organisation and selection of themes in a different manner.

CHECKPOINT:

1. *You need to study a minimum of five case studies for the HSC. They will be needed in both Section I and Section II of the HSC written Examination paper.*
2. *Your case studies should cover a variety of different themes, artists, art movements and issues.*
3. *The case studies should synthesise (merge) information about artists, artworks and art movements with your knowledge of Practice, the Conceptual Framework and the Frames.*

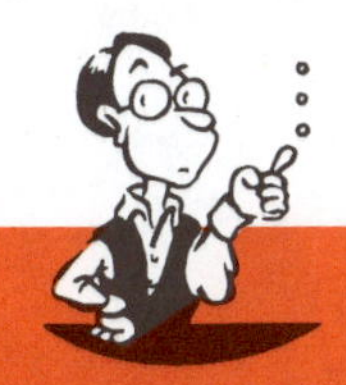

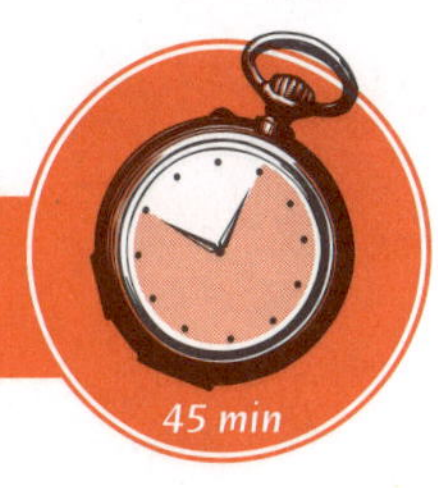

YOUR TOPIC INFO

The Body: From Caves to Virtual Reality

This case study is an investigation of the **historical representations of the body (figurative art)**, examining how **visual conventions and representations** have changed over time and how **ideological shifts** have influenced art practice. If studying this case study, students will come to understand the **differing forms of representation** that have been used throughout history.

This first case study by no means covers the entire history of art and does not intend to do so. Instead, it highlights **key art practices** and provides an opportunity to investigate **historical and critical aspects** of this theme. The **key areas** that could be selected for study might include:

- Palaeolithic cave paintings (The human form and primitive culture)
- Egyptian painting and sculpture (The human form and mythology)
- Greek sculpture (The classical figure)
- Gothic painting and sculpture (Religion and the human form)
- Renaissance painting and sculpture (Humanism and the depiction of the body)
- Romantic painting (The human form and the sublime)
- Photographic pictorialism (Early photographic portraiture)
- Impressionist painting and sculpture (Naturalism and figuration)
- Cubist painting (New ways of seeing the body)
- Expressionist painting (The figure and human emotions)
- Photorealism painting and sculpture (The impact of photography on art)
- Neo-expressionism (Postmodern painting and figuration)
- Performance and conceptual art (The body as an art object)
- **Feminist art** (The body in feminist art)
- Virtuality and digital media (Art and cyberbiogenetics).

On the following page is an example of how one of these key areas (**Feminist art**) might be investigated within the case study. This **Conceptual Framework diagram** and **Frames matrix** (over the page) could be applied to any of the **key areas** listed above. Alternatively, the material could be extended into its own case study on the body in feminist art.

The Body in Feminist Art: Conceptual Framework

FEMINIST ART

WORLD

- Mary Wollstonecraft's *A Vindication of the Rights of Woman* in 1792 outlines the needs for gender equity and social justice.
- In 1918, women are granted the right to vote in England as a result of the activity of the suffragettes.
- World War II (1939–45) sees a large population of women joining the work force to assist in the war effort.
- Simone de Beauvoir writes *The Second Sex* in 1949, providing an account of the conditions of women.
- Betty Friedan writes *The Feminine Mystique* in 1963 and forms the National Organisation of Women in 1966. This motivates women to question their role in society and critically assess their situation.
- During the late 1960s and 1970s, the feminist movement becomes known as Women's Liberation.
- During the late 1980s there is a recognised feminist backlash and a need for a new generation of feminists. Writers such as Naomi Wolf and Susan Faludi suggest the need to change political direction and become more critical about feminist issues.
- Issues concerning women's rights in different cultures become a priority with regard to gender and social equity.

ARTWORK

- Many artworks produced by female artists employ signs and symbols that outline the issues of femininity and feminism, such as motherhood, gender identity, gender equity and the uniqueness of females.
- Artemesia Gentileschi (c. 1593–1652), is a recognised female painter from the Renaissance period who has been identified through a feminist revision of art history.
- Judy Chicago's *The Dinner Party* (1974–79) highlights the importance of the historical representation of women, demonstrating how art can articulate feminist issues.
- Guerrilla Girls are a contemporary feminist art movement which seeks social, racial and gender equity within the artworld.
- Many contemporary artists deal with images that allude to the female body. This form of representation is known as essentialist imagery.

AUDIENCE

- Feminist writers such as Germaine Greer and Linda Nochlin outlined the need to review the history of art and analyse why female artists have been excluded from historical narratives about art.
- Postmodern feminists attempt to add a more critical dialogue, suggesting that feminism may have evolved into a 'post-feminism' movement that looks beyond gender issues. However, other contemporary feminists contest this and maintain the need for equity.
- Many female artists sought to make the audience aware of the inherent bias that has existed against women in the artworld.
- Through the visual expression of many female artists, the audience is made aware of the broad and diverse range of issues and concerns that are faced by female artists.
- In Australia in 1991, the *Frames of Reference* exhibition shows a retrospective of differing attitudes to feminism.
- Guerrilla Girls have used performance in their work to make the audience aware of racial or gender discrimination that occurs in the artworld.

ARTIST

- Barbara Kruger, Jenny Holzer, Guerrilla Girls and Maria Kozic are artists who have employed commercial forms of media for artistic expression, including billboards, Internet sites and advertisements.
- Physical and cultural concerns have been examined by artists to articulate their personal and public identities. Artists such as Rea, Judy Watson, Fiona Foley and Tracey Moffatt examine the identity of Australian indigenous women, while others such as Julie Rrap, Vanessa Beecroft, Janine Antoni, Judy Chicago and Cindy Sherman explore the identities of women in Western society.
- Performance artists such as Karen Finley, Penny Arcade, Linda Sproul and Laurie Anderson examine issues such as sexual identity, domestic violence and gender identities in their artworks.

The Body in Feminist Art: The Frames

Subjective Frame

Feminist artists were concerned with how they were perceived in the artworld. They often felt isolated, and dealt with issues that were not considered as important as the issues explored by male artists (e.g. Judy Chicago, Guerilla Girls, Barbara Kruger).

Structural Frame

Feminist and Marxist critics re-evaluated the conventions of representation of the female form throughout history.

Cultural Frame

Most cultures throughout history display a particular mode of representing the female form. The nude in western art has been firmly established as a legitimate convention, which differs from the eastern representation of the nude as seen in Japanese 'Shunga' prints.

Postmodern Frame

Post-feminist artists are evaluating the claims made by feminist artists of the 1970s and seeking to develop their own forms of representation. This can be seen in the work of Orlan, Tracey Emin, Gillian Wearing and Pipilotti Rist.

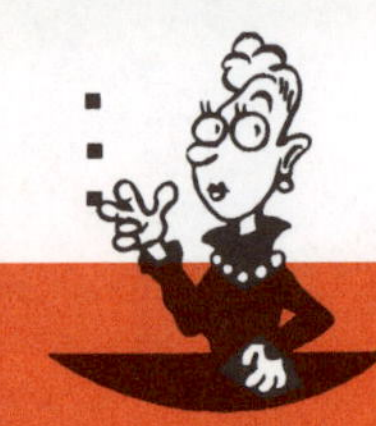

CASE STUDIES IN THE HSC
Further Case Studies

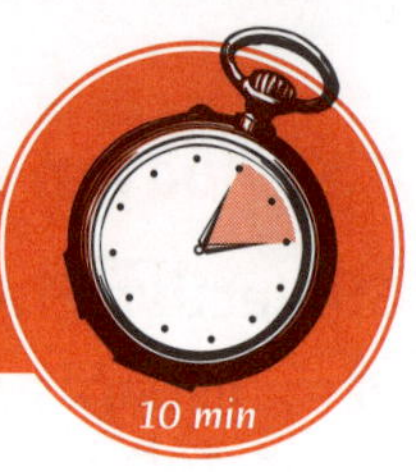

YOUR TOPIC INFO

Order/Chaos: Identifying the Difference Between Modern and Postmodern Art Practice

This case study investigates key art practitioners within modernism and postmodernism in terms of how they represent their worlds and how others have viewed them. The study explores the important characteristics that differentiate modernism and postmodernism.

Gallery Visit: Examining Aspects of Representation in an Exhibition

This case study involves going into an exhibition and using knowledge from previous case studies to assess the different representations. This example shows how your case studies can depend on each other for background information.

Australian Vision

This case study asks, 'What is Australian art?' through investigating Australia's indigenous, colonial and postcolonial identities.

Art and Technology

This study traces the relationship between technology and the evolution of practice (artmaking/history/criticism) in art.

Other Case Studies

Some ideas for further case studies you might study are:

- The Built Environment: examination of architecture
- Secular and Spiritual: the role of spirituality in art
- Abstraction: the philosophy and conventions of non-realistic art
- Art and Asia-Pacific: an examination of traditional and contemporary Asian art
- The Environment: assessing how different artists have interacted with the landscape
- Art and Politics: the impact of world events on the artworld
- Art and Public Spaces: an investigation into public art
- Inner Vision: the importance of subjectivity in art and how artists produce artworks.

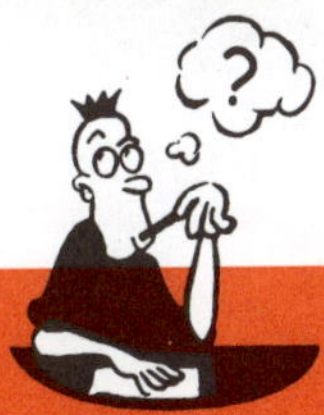

CASE STUDIES IN THE HSC

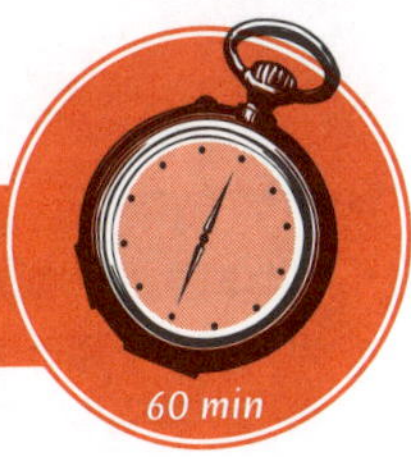

TEST YOUR KNOWLEDGE

1. What is the minimum number of case studies that must be studied for the HSC?

2. What does a case study set out to do?

3. Which parts of the HSC content (Practice, Conceptual Framework and Frames) do you have to examine in your case studies?

4. Do you need to have an understanding of the relevant art history and art criticism for each case study?

5. How important is it to understand the role and relationship between the artists, artwork, audience and world in your case study?

6. Name five important aspects of 'representation' in art.

7. On the following two pages is a grid that outlines the key elements of the Conceptual Framework (artist, artwork, audience and world) and asks you to define them in terms of the four Frames (Subjective, Structural, Cultural, Postmodern).

   Select a case study you have studied and see if you can answer the questions in the boxes for that case study. (You might want to draw up blank boxes in the same layout as shown here, then fill in the details in point form.)

   Note that you can use this grid to revise each of your case studies if you wish.

☞ *Answers on page 85*

Artist	
Subjective • What were the artist's **personal thoughts** and how are these represented in their approaches to artmaking? • What **intimate and private characteristics** are known about the artist? • How does the artist express their own **experiences**? • What **imaginative qualities** are produced by the artist?	**Structural** • Does the artist align the artmaking to a particular **style or theme**? Why? • Does the artist use a specific **visual language** that reveals and informs the audience about the artist's life and philosophy? • Are there **personal codes and symbols** used by the artist? What are they?
Cultural • Does the artist reflect the **beliefs and values** of society of the time? • Doest the artist reflect **cultural issues** in the artworks? • Is the understanding of the artist specific to a particular **culture**, or is it universal? • Does the artist's approach to artmaking reflect **cultural and historical** concerns?	**Postmodern** • If the artist is a contemporary practitioner, how has he or she been influenced by **postmodern theories**? • Does the artist use **postmodern conventions** such as parody, appropriation, recontextualisation or eclecticism? • How have **contemporary historians and critics** constructed meaning in the artworks?

Artwork	
Subjective • How does the artwork sum up the **experiences and ideas** of the artist? • How is the artwork a **bridge** between the artist and the audience? • What **emotive response** does the artwork provoke? Why?	**Structural** • How does the artwork convey ideas through the use of use of **signs and symbols**? • What **artistic conventions** are specific to this artwork? • Is there a specific **art movement or style** identified with the artwork?
Cultural • Does the artwork highlight a **cultural event, issue or person**? What is the significance of this representation? • Is the artwork a **cultural artefact** that reveals significant ideas about the culture in which it was made and the time it was produced? How? • Does the artwork offer a **window** to the time and place in which it was produced? • How do **historians and critics** from **different cultures** examine and explain the importance of the artwork?	**Postmodern** • Is the artwork **postmodern**? Why or why not? • If the artwork is historical, how have **postmodern artists, historians and critics** related to the artwork? • What is the artwork's relationship to concepts of **originality, style, authority** and **readership**?

Audience	
Subjective • How does the **taste and education** of the audience influence the way they understand the artworks and artist(s)? • How important is an **emotional response** to an artwork? • Has the audience been **divided** in their assessment of the artworks or exhibitions relevant to your case study? Why?	**Structural** • How can the viewer recognise particular **styles and conventions** found within artworks?
Cultural • What kinds of audiences have viewed the artworks? • If the works are historical, what was the culture of **art audiences of the time**? Was there patronage of artists by the wealthy? • How have the different cultures of **audiences** influenced the way the artwork has been received?	**Postmodern** • What are the expectations of a **contemporary audience**? • What **specialists** are there in the contemporary world of the audience? • What is the role of the **curator**?

World	
Subjective • How influential is the world on the **emotional and imaginative qualities** of the audience and artist? • Are the spiritual, psychological, emotive and aesthetic sensibilities of the audience and artist related to **world events**? How?	**Structural** • Technology is specific to the times and places in which art is created. It also depends on the importance that the artworld has placed on such inventions in the evolution of art through history. What **inventions or use of technology** are specific to the case study?
Cultural • **Ideological aspects** such as religion, society, education and politics influence art. How have these shaped approaches to the art in your case study? • The ***zeitgeist* (spirit of the time)** reflects particular cultural qualities that are reflected in art. How is this evident in artworks? • What **value** does art maintain in the world in which your case study is situated?	**Postmodern** • How does the treatment of art in the **contemporary world** differ from its treatment in **historical or modern worlds**? • What **events** have radically shaped contemporary thought and how have they influenced current art practices?

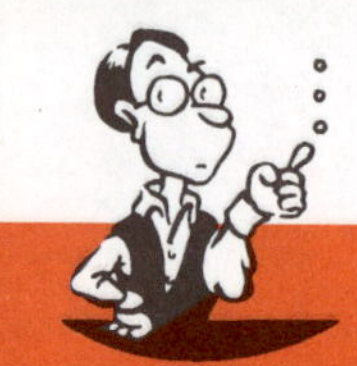

TIPS FOR THE HSC WRITTEN EXAMINATION

Preparing for the HSC Written Examination

It is a pretty daunting task to distill all the Visual Arts information you have studied and gathered over the years of your schooling and cram it into 90 minutes of written responses—but that is the structure of the course. The first word of advice is **don't panic!** This book should make you more familiar with the **structure** of the exam, which will prepare you and make you feel more confident.

There are **three important elements** to consider when approaching the HSC Visual Arts written Examination paper. They are:

- the **outcomes** outlined in the syllabus
- the **rubric** (the brief guidelines stated in the examination paper)
- the **questions** you answer.

A clear understanding of how these components interrelate will assist you in your preparation for the examination.

The Outcomes

The outcomes for the HSC content—Practice (Art History and Art Criticism), Conceptual Framework, Frames and Representation (meaning your case studies)—are found the syllabus (outcomes H7, H8, H9 and H10). These outline what you should be able to do by the completion of the course and will guide the examiners in setting the exam questions. It is worth going to the syllabus and looking at the specific outcomes, but here is a summary of what you should be able to do:

- Understand the practice of **art history and criticism**.
- Employ an understanding of the **Conceptual Framework** to appropriately outline the relationship of the artwork, audience, artists and world.
- Show how the **Frames** (Subjective/Structural/Cultural/Postmodern) can be used to give an understanding of critical and historical studies of art.
- Develop a **body of information** (case studies) about different representations of art, including historical material, critical material and other written accounts of artists and artworks.

The Rubric

The **rubric** appears at the **top of each section** of the HSC written Examination paper. It outlines how your written response will be assessed and provides a **checklist** for you as it highlights key points that must be included in your response. It is specific in its requirements and **must not be ignored**. It will include such requirements as:

- **Write in a concise and well-reasoned way**

  This is asking you to be **brief, to the point** and to show your knowledge and understanding on the subject in a logical fashion.

- **Present an informed point of view**

  To show that you are 'informed' requires you to demonstrate a knowledge of what you have learned in your **case studies** and apply your understanding of the **content** (Practice/Conceptual Framework/Frames) to this knowledge. Don't just use complex words without understanding what they mean. Instead, write in a clear and articulate manner that best conveys your knowledge and understanding.

- **Use the plates and any other source material provided to inform your response**

  This requires you to make **specific reference** to any **images supplied** (commonly called 'plates' in the examination paper), and any other **source material** such as **text extracts or quotes**. To ignore an image or source material will mean you are not fulfilling the criteria of the question and **cannot be awarded full marks**. Make sure you respond to whatever images are specifically mentioned in the question.

The Exam Questions

Section I is divided into three questions. The values of the questions will vary. Generally Question 1 will be the easiest and marks will be incremental in value with Question 2 and Question 3. A basic rule in terms of time is to allow roughly two minutes for each mark. So you might spend 5 minutes for 3 marks, 10 minutes for 5 marks, 20 minutes for 10 marks, and so on.

- **Demands of the question:** This refers to **exactly what is being asked**. Words such as *examine, discuss, outline* and *infer* are used as key demands within questions. Each word will have a particular demand. It is important that you understand what is requested. For a list of these words and their meanings, search 'glossary of key words' on the NESA website at www.educationstandards.nsw.edu.au.
- **Criteria of the question:** This relates to what **component of the HSC course content** is being examined. The question could be asking you about Practice, Conceptual Framework or Frames, or a more specific aspect of one of these. It is important to identify the criteria so you know which part of your knowledge to apply.
- **Context:** Sometimes a question will provide **hints or prompts** which are given to assist you in developing a response. Even the way a question is **phrased** may supply you with a context from which to develop your response. The **selection of images** for your response also offers a context to develop an answer.

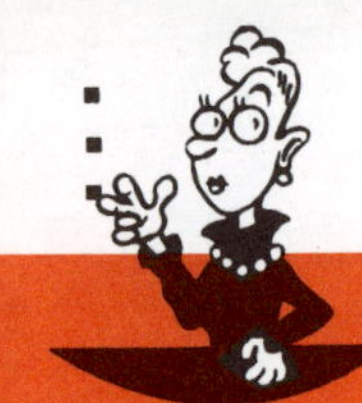

TIPS FOR THE HSC EXAMINATION

Responding to Examination Questions

Familiarising yourself with these three elements will give you more confidence in the exam.

Section I: Question 1

- Question 1 generally has a low mark value (up to **5 marks**).
- This will be an **fairly straightforward** question. You should be able to respond to it without much difficulty.
- Make sure you identify **which part of the content** the question addresses (Practice/Conceptual Framework/Frames).
- It may only ask for a **specific piece of information** dealing with only one part of a focus area. For example, a Practice question might supply an image of an artwork and ask you to comment on the way the artist has approached their artmaking.
- Be **brief**: make sure each sentence states a **relevant point** and don't repeat yourself—you simply will not have the time.
- Remember to address the demands of the **rubric** that appears at the top of the examination paper (see page 67). This provides you with an outline of how you are expected to structure your responses.
- You are expected to spend **10 minutes** answering this question.

Section I: Question 2

- Question 2 generally has a medium mark value.
- The level of difficulty will increase and require a **greater engagement** with the question. You will need to demonstrate a deeper understanding of the content.
- **More than one image** may be used in this question.
- Again, keep each point you make **relevant to the question**. You have a little more time to answer this one, but not long enough to run off on a tangent. Try to make all the points you want to make as clearly and succinctly as you can.
- You are expected to spend **15 minutes** answering this question.

Section I: Question 3

- Question 3 generally has a higher mark value.

- This will be a more **demanding question**. In this response you need to demonstrate a comprehensive understanding of what the question is asking you to do. This is the most challenging question of Section I.
- You need to ensure that you answer what the question is asking and recognise what part of the **content** the question is assessing (Practice/Conceptual Framework/Frames).
- A number of **images plus text samples** may be used in the question. The **rubric** will tell you to use **all images and text** in your response, so make sure you do so—to ignore the rubric will cost you marks.
- In this question you are expected to develop a **well thought-out** and insightful response.
- Any examples you use from your **case studies** will need to be correctly sourced and used to back up your arguments, not just thrown in to pad out your response.
- Make **clear reference to the question** and respond in an explicit and concise manner.
- You need to show that you can **merge** your knowledge of the syllabus content with the sample artworks and text provided in the question.
- You are expected to spend **20 minutes** answering this question.

TIP! It is a good idea to practise writing for 10, 15 and 20 minute blocks so you know how much you are able to write in these time limits. Be mindful, however, that the mark value can change for each Section I–type question. You don't want to end up with a shortened amount of time to answer your Section II question.

Section II Questions

Section II requires you to write an **extended-response** answer to one of the six questions (Questions 4–9) you are offered. Three questions for each area of HSC content (Practice/Conceptual Framework/Frames) will be offered. You are expected to spend **45 minutes** answering this question.

- **Guessing** the type of question that may appear in Section II will be good practice in your preparation. You should be able to nominate what **type of question** you will answer:
  - **Practice**: If you find that your research covers analysis of **artists' intentions** and artmaking practices, and evaluates how historians and critics have developed understanding of artworks, then questions relating to the Practice area would be suitable.
  - **Conceptual Framework**: If you find you are good at **making links** between the different **parts of the artworld** (artists, artwork, audience and world)

and how they impact upon the production of artworks, then a Conceptual Framework question might be good for you.

- **Frames**: If you are more prone to analysing artists and artworks in terms of how they can be **interpreted**, then perhaps the Frames would be a suitable area to prepare for Section II.

- Identifying a specific area to respond to in Section II is a good idea in preparation for this component of the exam, but **be careful**. With all meticulous planning and pre-empting of the types of questions that could be in the exam, you might find that the three questions offered in your nominated area of content may be **too difficult to answer**. So ensure you can adjust your information into other areas with ease.

- For example, you might have been preparing to respond to a question based upon the Conceptual Framework, but in the actual exam these types of questions do not offer you the scope to reflect your thorough knowledge of the subject. Look at the **Practice** or **Frames** questions and see if there's a more appropriate one which will be able to reflect your knowledge. You will need to be flexible in your preparation and identify the best ways to convey your understanding of the subject through the careful and considered selection of a question.

  TIP! If you find in the exam you have to adjust your knowledge to suit a different area of content, make sure you **answer the question you are given**. Don't just answer the question you would have *liked* to see in the exam! A good way to start off on the right track is to specifically address and define the **words and terms used in the question**, and follow this through your essay. It is one thing to have a wealth of knowledge about the visual arts, but another thing to be able to write this information in an appropriate manner. You will need to know **how to write an essay** and how to identify **what is being asked** in the question.

And remember ... practice makes perfect!

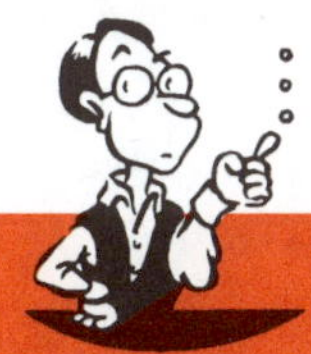

TIPS FOR THE HSC EXAMINATION

Essay Writing Tips for Section II

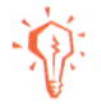

TIP 1: Know Your Subject

Make sure you are familiar with the **case studies** you have studied and try to connect them to your knowledge of the **content**: Practice, the Conceptual Framework and the Frames.

TIP 2: Remember Your Essay Technique

Make sure that when you write your Section II extended-response answer, you use good essay-writing technique.

- Your **introduction** should outline how you will respond to the question. Don't just repeat the question, but map out your response in a way that highlights your understanding of the question and your intentions in the essay.
- Each paragraph in the **body** of the essay should have key points made in a succinct (concise, not too wordy) manner. The first sentence in each paragraph should act as a topic sentence which outlines the points of the paragraph. Then add your explanation and examples to support the main point of the paragraph.
- The **conclusion** should sum up all the key points. Don't make new points here: the conclusion is meant to be a unifying feature that sums up all the important points made in the essay.

TIP 3: Use Good Examples

Select and discuss **artists, artworks, critics and historians** that are relevant to the question. Use examples to support your points and apply your knowledge to the specific question you are asked.

Use **primary quotes and references** to enrich your response. Demonstrate to the marker how you can appropriately apply references from critics and historians.

TIP 4: Keep it Relevant

Develop and maintain a **coherent point of view**. Ensure that your answer stays focused on the question and doesn't wander from this focus.

TIP 5: Use Appropriate Language

Writing about art requires you to employ **specific terms and language** relevant to the question. Demonstrating your knowledge of specific terminology and vocabulary will help you construct a good essay.

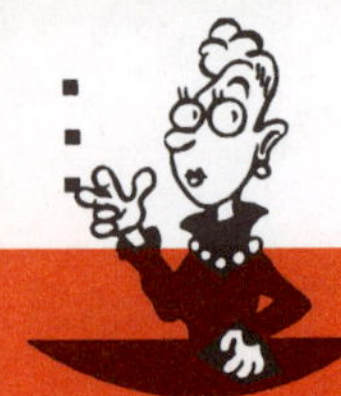

TIPS FOR THE HSC EXAMINATION

General Tips

TIP 1: Don't Panic!

The images that are used in the exam may not be familiar to you. The way the questions are structured may not be what you expected. However, be confident that the synthesis of what you have learnt in your **case studies** and your revision of the **core content** should be enough to see you through.

TIP 2: Allocate Your Time

Each question in the exam is worth a **certain number of marks**. Spend **more time** on the questions worth more marks. Use the times suggested on pages 68–69 to guide you.

TIP 3: Make it Relevant

Most importantly, **answer the question**. At the top of both Sections I and II of the paper will be some guidelines (**rubric**) which explain what features of your answers you will be assessed on ('In your answers you will be assessed on how well you ...'). **Read these guidelines**, and make your responses **relevant** to them.

TIP 4: Practice Makes Perfect

Make sure you practise answering questions **under exam conditions** to see how much you can write in the time allowed. The more familiar you are with the format and the timing of the exam, the more confident you will be.

TIP 5: Write on the Lines!

Use only the **lined paper** in the examination booklet to write your answers. The **blank pages** are only for planning and preparation.

TIP 6: Read Over Your Answers

If you have time, make sure you **reread your responses**. If you need to add another point, try using some form of footnote citation.

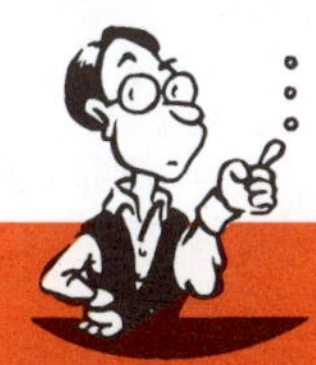

TIPS FOR THE HSC EXAMINATION

Key Words in Examination Questions

The NSW Education Standards Authority (NESA) has put together a **list of words** used in HSC written Examination questions. The following words are included on the list: it would be a good idea to familiarise yourself with what they mean when they appear in a Visual Arts question.

For the complete list, see the **NESA website**.

Word	What it is asking you to do
account for	state reasons for; report on
analyse	identify components and the relationship between them; draw out and relate implications
assess	make a judgement of value, quality, outcomes, results or size
clarify	make clear or plain
compare	show how things are similar or different
critically (analyse/ evaluate)	add a degree or level of accuracy, depth, knowledge and understanding, logic, questioning, reflection and quality to
define	provide characteristics and features
describe	outline and articulate the distinguishing features
discuss	identify issues and provide points for and/or against
evaluate	make a judgement based on criteria; determine the value of
examine	inquire into
explain	relate cause and effect; make the relationships between things evident; provide why and/or how
identify	recognise and name
interpret	draw meaning from
investigate	plan, inquire into and draw conclusions about
justify	support an argument or conclusion

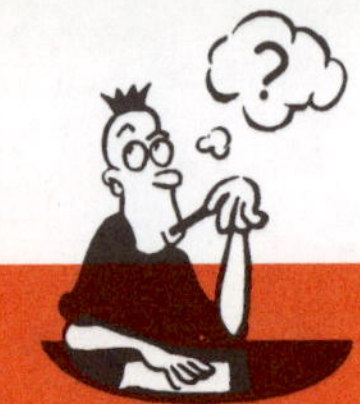

SAMPLE HSC EXAMINATION PAPER

General Instructions

- Reading time—5 minutes
- Working time—1½ hours

Section I

Total marks: 25

Attempt all parts of Question 1.

Allow about 45 minutes for this section:

- 10 minutes for Question 1
- 15 minutes for Question 2
- 20 minutes for Question 3.

In your answers you will be assessed on how well you:

- write in a concise and well-reasoned way
- present an informed point of view
- use the plates and any other source material provided to inform your response.

Question 1 (5 marks)

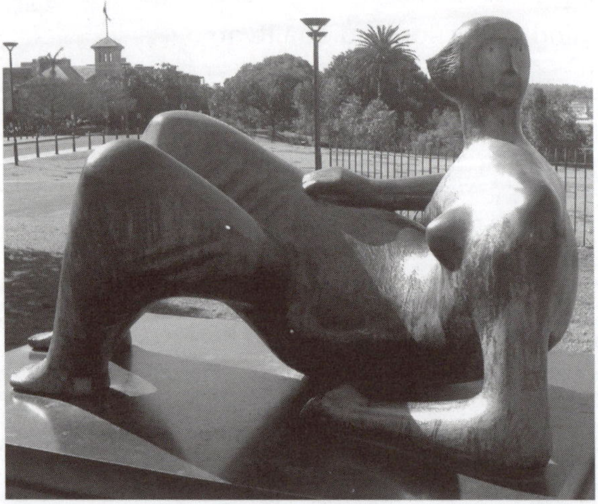

Plate 1: Henry Moore, *Reclining Figure*, 1935–36
Bronze cast, 48.3 cm x 89 cm x 38 cm

What comments can be made on the artist's personal perception of the subject?

☞ *Answers on page 99*

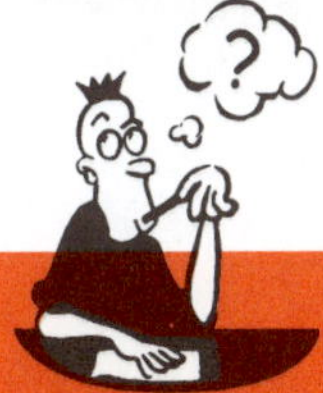

Question 2

How do these artworks (Plates 1, 2 and 3) communicate ideas about the artists' worlds? (8 marks)

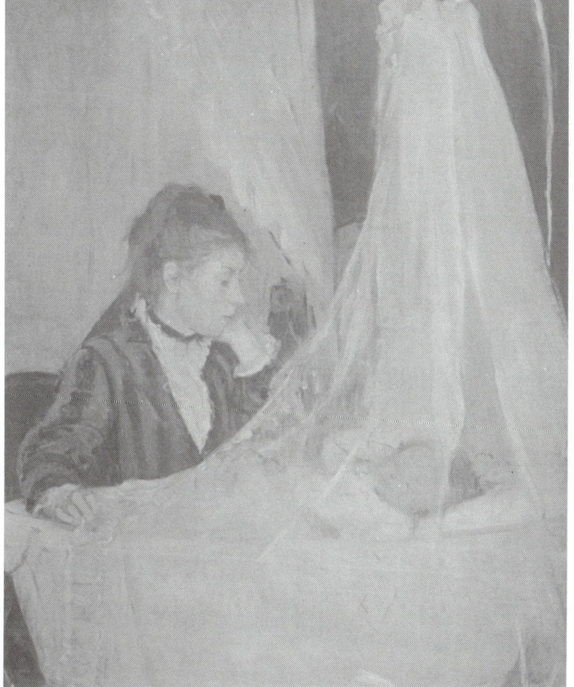

Plate 1: Berthe Morisot, *La Cuna*, 1872
Oil on canvas, 56 cm x 46 cm

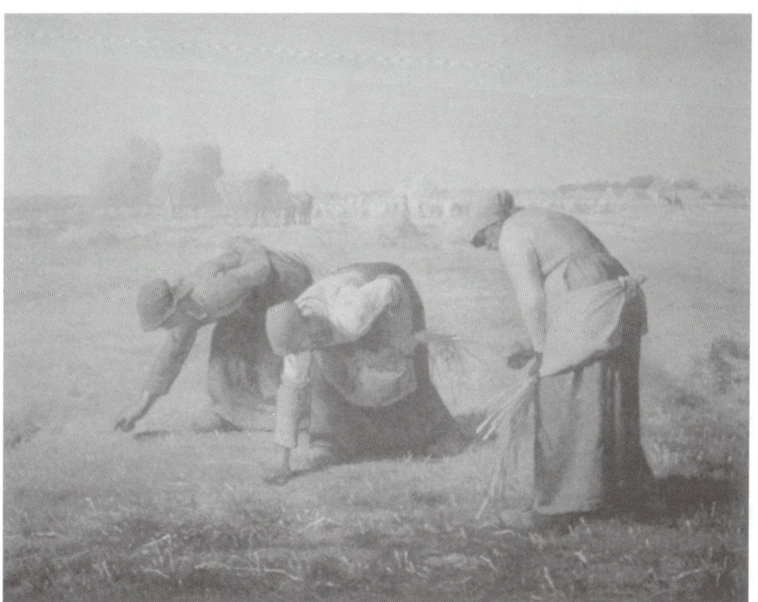

Plate 2: Jean-François Millet, *Les Glaneuses (The Gleaners)*, 1857
Oil on canvas,
83.5 cm x 111 cm

☞ *Answers on page 99*

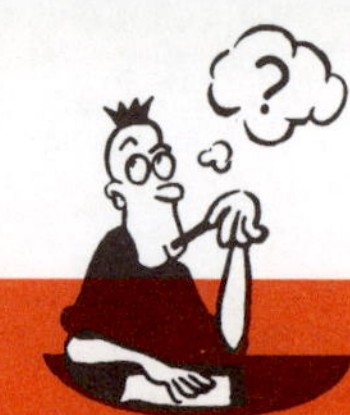

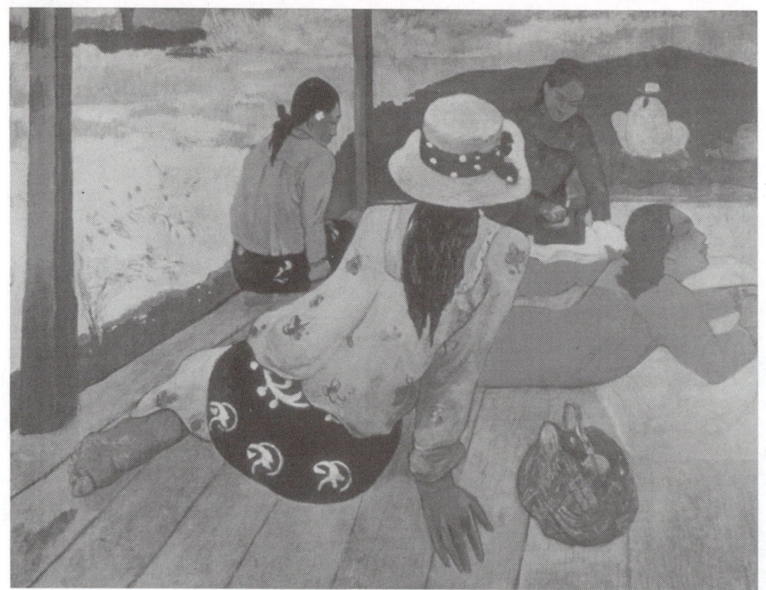

Plate 3: Paul Gauguin, *The Siesta,* c. 1892–94 Oil on canvas, 88.9 cm x 116.2 cm

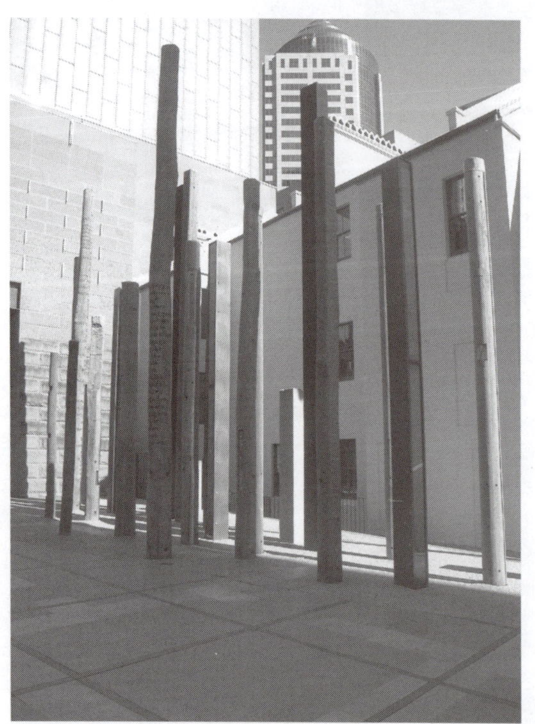

Plate 4: Janet Laurence and Fiona Foley, *Edge of the Trees: A Sculptural Installation*, 1994–95. Wood, sandstone, steel and found objects

☞ *Answers on page 99*

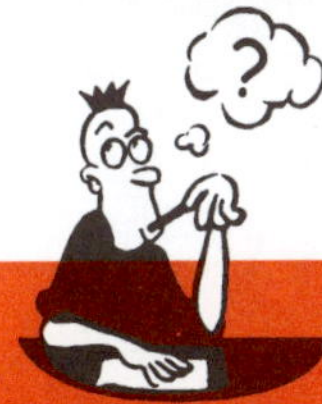

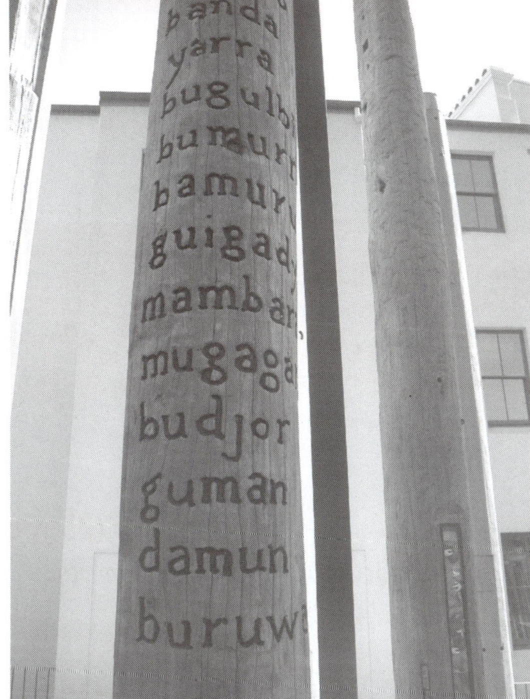

Plate 5: *Edge of the Trees* (detail)

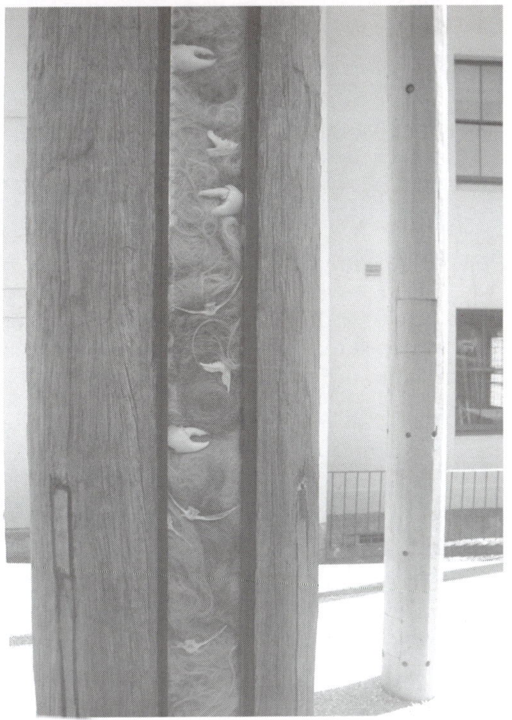

Plate 6: *Edge of the Trees* (detail)

Fiona Foley and Janet Laurence produced a collaborative installation work that greets the people as they enter the Museum of Sydney. It is an installation that reflects post-colonial concerns, primarily dealing with Australia's reconciliation with the past and the potential cultural development in the future. It is a unique installation that provides an aural, textural and visual experience as it assembles a critical account of the European colonisation of Australia.

Question 3

Look at Plates 4, 5 and 6 and the text extract. Evaluate the importance of history and events in the production of this artwork. (12 marks)

☞ *Answers on page 99*

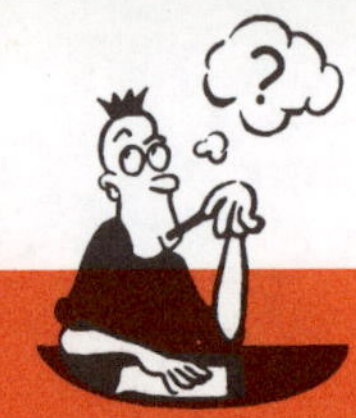

Section II

Total marks: 25

Attempt ONE question from Questions 4–9.

Allow about 45 minutes for this section.

In your answer you will be assessed on how well you:
- present a well-reasoned and informed point of view
- apply your understandings of the different aspects of content as appropriate (Practice, Conceptual Framework, and the Frames)
- use relevant examples.

PRACTICE

Question 4 (25 marks)

Discuss the importance of ideas in influencing the production of artworks.

OR

Question 5 (25 marks)

Discuss how artists have differed in their practice over time. Use examples to support your answer.

THE CONCEPTUAL FRAMEWORK

Question 6 (25 marks)

'Without an audience there could be no art.'

Discuss this statement in terms of the relationship of the audience to the artwork and artist.

OR

Question 7 (25 marks)

'Artists interact with the events and issues of their time and place.'

Discuss this statement and examine how the world is represented by artists in their artworks.

☞ *Answers on pages 100–105*

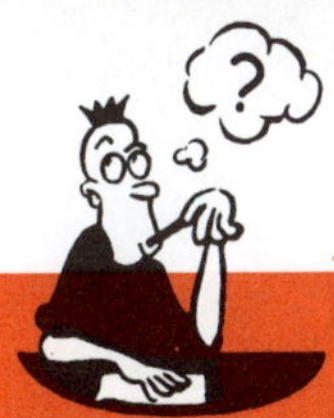

FRAMES

Question 8 (25 marks)

'Meaning in artworks and understanding artists' intentions will always be dependent on the cultures the artists come from.'

Discuss, making reference to artists and artworks you have studied.

OR

Question 9 (25 marks)

'Postmodern art challenges all conventions within art—even the legitimacy of itself.'

Do you agree with this statement? Give reasons and specific examples in your response.

END OF PAPER

☞ *Answers on pages 105–107*

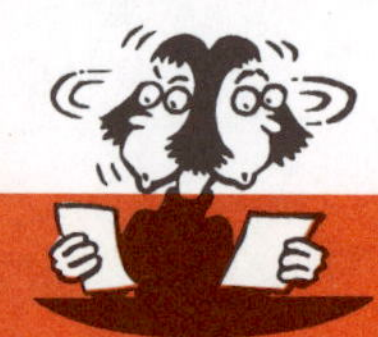

ANSWERS—TEST YOUR KNOWLEDGE

ARTMAKING–THE BODY OF WORK

ARTMAKING IN THE HSC

Page 17

1. The body of work can be a variety of things. Most importantly, it is a collection of one or more artworks that represents your interests and skills, and communicates in a visual and conceptual manner. There are no definite ways of defining a BOW, as it will vary from person to person. It can be prepared using a range of different expressive forms.

2. Technical resolution refers to the qualities and aspects of refinement that are demonstrated in the BOW. It is the development and mastery of the material you are using in your artmaking and refers to how well you handle and use the material in an artistic manner.

3. Conceptual strength and meaning is conveyed through how well your ideas and concepts are conveyed in your BOW. Thinking about what to select for the BOW, and how well each piece (if there is more than one) complements and sustains the overall idea of the work will give your work these qualities. If your intentions are not clear, this reflects poor conceptual strength and resolution of ideas. If there is a certainty and engagement with the audience of your work, this suggests there is a high level of conceptual strength and meaning.

4. The term 'expressive form' refers to the media you use in your BOW. The choices of expressive forms are:
   - Drawing
   - Graphic design
   - Scuplture
   - Collection of works
   - Painting
   - Time-based forms
   - Ceramics
   - Photomedia
   - Printmaking
   - Documented forms
   - Textiles and fibres
   - Designed objects and environments

5. The weight restriction is 35 kg, and not a gram more!

6. Individual works must not exceed two square metres, with a total surface area of six square metres. A work larger than two square metres and under six square metres must be either rolled up or hinged if it is a singular piece. They can be multiple pieces provided no one piece exceeds 2 square metres.

7. The maximum volumetric measurement for a BOW when displayed is one cubic metre. This must also takes into account negative space that surrounds the object.

8. Hypodermic needles, syringes, blood products and bodily secretions. Also as a general rule anything that could cut or harm the maker who is handling the BOW. Other dangerous and sharp objects such as broken glass, barbed wire and nails should not be used.

9. The BOW mark is worth 50% of the HSC Visual Arts mark.

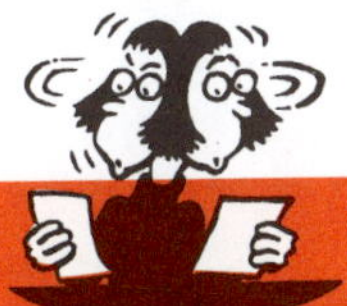

ANSWERS—TEST YOUR KNOWLEDGE

10 The VAPD is a place for collecting images and information, experimenting, documenting your artmaking process, sounding out your ideas and revisiting them later.

CONTENT

PRACTICE IN ARTMAKING, ART CRITICISM & ART HISTORY

Page 28

1 The three areas are artmaking, art criticism and art history.

2 Studying these aspects is important so that we recognise how these activities contribute to the knowledge and existence of the visual arts. Through the study of artmaking, art history and art criticism you will understand how viewpoints, actions and concepts are produced, and the factors which influence them.

3 Here are some examples of important issues in artmaking. You may have others.
- Representation of thoughts, feelings, ideas and experiences
- Development of stylistic innovations
- Use of emerging technologies
- Use of personal/social symbols and signs
- Treatment and use of materials in the development of an artwork
- How the artwork can be interpreted
- The purpose and intention of the artist

4 The purpose of art criticism is to clarify and assess artworks and the actions of artists. The critic offers evaluations and explanations to enable others to understand the visual arts.

5 Compare your answer to this list on page 22. Three of the important points are:
- Critics provide a comprehensive account of an artwork.
- They explain what is significant in/about an artwork.
- They establish relevance between the artwork and the audience.

6 Art history maps out the significance of artworks and artists in relation to their contexts—the periods of time and the places in which they worked. It uses historical research and analysis to find meaning(s) in artworks.

7 Four important considerations for art history are:
- suggesting how historical events affected both society and individual artists of the time
- providing accounts of how artists, styles and artworks evolve
- identifying and explaining the cultural qualities that influence the production of an artwork
- explaining characteristic features of historical works to a contemporary audience.

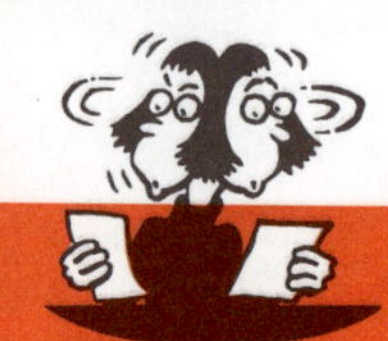

ANSWERS—TEST YOUR KNOWLEDGE

8. To be able to interpret and judge artworks using art criticism and art history, you first need to have a comprehensive understanding of the artworks and artists. The more you know about the subject, the more informed your interpretation will be, and the more selective you can be about providing a critical or historical account of an artwork. Interpretation and judgement are very important but they must be informed by a knowledge of the practice of art history and art criticism.

THE CONCEPTUAL FRAMEWORK—AGENCIES IN THE ARTWORLD

Page 39

1. The Conceptual Framework outlines the 'who, what, when and why' of the artworld by looking at the relationship of its four main components: the artist, the artwork, the world and the audience. It examines the causes and effects of events in the artworld.

2. The artist:
   - is the producer who makes the artworks and creates a particular way of looking at the world through their mode of interpretation.

   The artwork:
   - is the work produced by the artist (can be material, physical and virtual objects)
   - refers to pieces of evidence that give an account of what the artist was thinking and feeling.

   The world:
   - refers to the time and place in which the artist lived or when the artwork is being viewed
   - highlights that world events, social and cultural outlooks and other factors can also have an influence on the other agents of the artworld.

   The audience:
   - is the 'critical consumers' of artworks: those who interpret, judge and validate the artworks and acknowledge the impact of the artist
   - brings meaning to artworks and art movements
   - includes those educated about art, such as students, teachers, critics, historians, curators, patrons (those who give money and funding to artists) and theorists, but also refers to the general public.

3. The audience can include those listed above: general public, students, teachers, critics, theorists, historians, curators and patrons.

4. You will obviously need to choose your own example here. The following is a sample answer using the artist Marcel Duchamp.

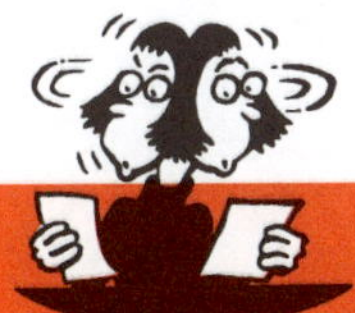

ANSWERS—TEST YOUR KNOWLEDGE

Artist(s)	Marcel Duchamp (1887–1968) • Radicalised the modern art world through a number of artmaking practices generated by the spirit of the *avant garde.* • Challenged aesthetic conditions of the time with the introduction of 'readymades'—everyday objects presented as works of art. • Disputed the tastes of the 'bourgeoisie', who were the dominant buyers of art at that time. • Gave up art as a futile exercise to play chess in the early 1920s.
Artworks	*Fountain*, 1917 *Nude Descending a Staircase*, 1912 *The Bride Stripped Bare by her Bachelors, Even,* 1915–23 • Each of these artworks shows a radical way of looking at the world. • The idea of art being beautiful to the eye is being ridiculed. • The artworks highlight the conceptual concerns of the artist. • Such artworks would radically revolutionise the artworld and lay the foundations for postmodern art.
Audience	• The audience at the time was shocked. • The 'readymade' work *Fountain* was originally thrown away by gallery organisers, as they misunderstood the intention of the artist (it was recreated in the 1960s). • Later the shock of the 'readymades' would be appreciated and influence other conceptual artists of the 1970s. • Many art theorists view Duchamp as a key figure who changed the direction of modern art.
World	• The world was being radically changed through the mechanisation of the workforce. • Communications and transport made distant places more easily accessible. • World War I (1914–1918) was seen by many artists as a complete catastrophe and made them question the values and attitudes of modern society.

5 This diagram will be based on one of your own case studies. This is a good way to revise part of your case study.

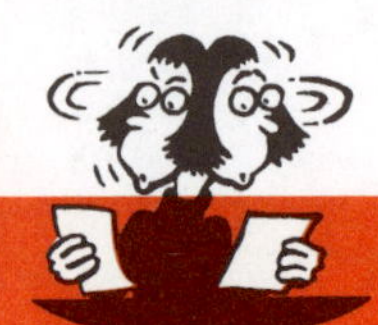

ANSWERS—TEST YOUR KNOWLEDGE

THE FRAMES

Page 52

These are some examples. You may have others.

1. The **Subjective Frame** looks at:
   - the feelings and experiences communicated by the artworks
   - the emotional responses which the work is trying to get from the audience
   - the psychological concerns that are communicated in the artwork, both consciously and unconsciously.

   The **Structural Frame** looks at:
   - the governing aesthetic principles of the artwork—how the artwork is constructed in terms of particular rules and conventions
   - the use of symbols and signs/codes to convey specific ideas about the subject matter
   - the communicative value of an artwork—how well the artist uses the codes and conventions to express their ideas.

   The **Cultural Frame** looks at:
   - the values and beliefs of the society where the artist/artwork originates, and how these can influence both the creation of art and the way it is received by an audience
   - any political significance which might be found in an artwork, and how political issues might have affected the artist
   - the way in which the artist is both a chronicler and a critic of cultural identity and the actions of society.

   The **Postmodern Frame**:
   - challenges traditional modes of thinking and representation in art
   - questions the absolute rules about aesthetics, dominant styles and recognised conventions
   - uses approaches to artmaking such as appropriation, irony, eclecticism and recontextualisation to create artworks that challenge ideas about originality and make the audience question their own expectations.

2. Personal or 'subjective' qualities refer to the unique and imaginative way an artist has interpreted subject matter or conveyed an idea. Each artist will develop a personal style and unique approach to artmaking, and will use this to express their intentions and feelings.

3. Signs and symbols are objects and images that hold specific meaning to the artist and audience. Some artists will use very public symbols; for example, the Cubist painter Picasso used the bull to represent masculinity and virility. A symbol will stand in the place of an idea or a concept, while a sign provides an immediate identification and direction to meaning.

4. Postmodernism is a term which describes the art theories and practices of the late twentieth century onwards. It is a contemporary situation where the artworld questions all accepted rules and norms and becomes critical about the whole process of artmaking and looking

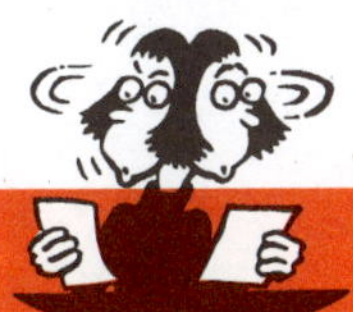

ANSWERS—TEST YOUR KNOWLEDGE

at art. It highlights that meaning in an artwork will depend on how the audience views and interprets it. Postmodernism attempts to be critical of the past and also of itself.

5 Cultural influence relates to the values and beliefs of a society at a specific time and place.

CASE STUDIES IN THE HSC

Page 63

1 You must study at least five case studies for the HSC.

2 Case studies aim to give you in-depth knowledge of artists, artworks and art movements. They ensure that your knowledge of the HSC content (Practice, Conceptual Framework and the Frames) is applied to real-life examples.

3 You have to examine *all* of the HSC content. The degree to which you apply particular areas of the content will depend on the focus of the case study. However, by the end of the five case studies you should have a thorough knowledge of applying the Practice, Conceptual Framework and Frames areas to the particular artists, movements and artworks you have studied.

4 Yes, you do. Art criticism and art history is part of the Practice area of content. You need to understand the critical ideas and historical information to give your case study the appropriate context.

5 Very important! This is a crucial part of taking a wholistic approach to your case study, rather than studying an artist in a 'vacuum'. These elements are the four 'agencies in the artworld' discussed in the Conceptual Framework. You must understand the relationships between them to fully understand your case study.

6 Five of: styles, themes, genres, critical theories, historical narratives, use of technology and aesthetic conventions.

7 This will depend on the case study you choose. It's a good way to test or revise your knowledge of a particular case study with reference to the four frames.

ANSWERS—KEY EXAM QUESTIONS

The answers provided are simply guidelines for your answers; yours may differ from these. You need to keep in mind the marks allocated for each type of question and adjust the length of your answers accordingly. Make sure you can justify your answers in a 'well-reasoned' way, and provide enough information from your case studies when needed.

PRACTICE IN ARTMAKING, ART CRITICISM & ART HISTORY

Page 29

1. Discuss the intentions of the artist in Plate 1.
   - Ingres wants to depict beauty.
   - He wants to realistically capture the human form.
   - The painting provides a voyeuristic account of the female form.
   - He seems fascinated by the exotic qualities of the East.
   - We see a celebration of the artist's skills with this medium. (5 marks)

2. Account for the approaches in artmaking in Plate 1.
   - He is concerned with realism—that is, with depicting the human form realistically.
   - Note the use of theatrical lighting and placement of the figure.
   - There is a refined treatment of tone and a thorough knowledge of anatomy. (5 marks)

3. Critically assess Plate 1.
   - This is a treatment of the human figure.
   - It shows secular (non-religious) qualities of the female form.
   - It reflects the genre and it treatment during its time of production, reflecting qualities of the Romantic period.
   - You might refer to critics such as Kenneth Clark or John Berger who discuss the use of the nude in painting. (5 marks)

4. Account for key ideas found in Plate 1.
   Some ideas:
   - You could provide a brief formal critique here which discusses the accomplishment and treatment of paint.
   - You could write a short feminist critique, which will outline the patriarchal underpinnings attributed to this artwork.
   - You might focus on the artist's interest in 'orientalism' or the East. (5 marks)

5. How does Plate 1 offer a 'window' into the past?
   - It shows the way in which nude figures were stylised.
   - It highlights the treatment, composition and conventions that are used in the representation of the nude.
   - The colonisation of other worlds by European countries which occurred around the time of this painting offers an insight into the 'oriental' nature of the work. (5 marks)

6. Looking at Plate 1, discuss the historical significance of the artwork.
   - It shows the transition of the human from from spiritual (religious) to secular (non-religious) depiction.

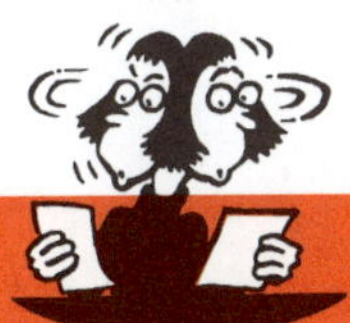

- It shows how artworks are shifting away from ownership of the church and state to individuals
- It indicates the fascination of artists of the time with exotic and romantic subject matter. (5 marks)

7 Look at Plates 2 and 3. Give an account of the importance of materials in the development of each artist's approach to artmaking.
- The postmodern convention of appropriation of materials—taking an object or material and using it for something other than its original purpose—is used.
- Photographic and digital technology has been used to create new images.
- Discuss the recontexualisation of artworks—putting something from a different context (time and/or place) into a new one. (8 marks)

8 Discuss the influence of the audience and world on the artist's approach to artmaking. Refer to Plates 2, 3 and 4 in your response.
- These artworks encourage the audience to rethink ideas about originality.
- They offer a critical view or 'critical dialogue' with the world of the past.
- They reveal the similarities and differences between the past and present. (8 marks)

9 Explain how art criticism provides better understanding of artworks. You must refer to Plates 2, 3 and 4 in your answer.
- An art critic with a knowledge of postmodernism would be able to discuss the importance of appropriation as a convention in these works. This would enable an audience to understand the technique.
- Art criticism can provide a clearer understanding of the signs and symbols used by the artists to convey their ideas.
- Criticism is important to be able to recognise the different approaches and conventions within the visual arts. (8 marks)

10 Look at Plates 2, 3 and 4. Give an account of how ideas about artmaking change over time.
- Discuss the use of appropriation as the basis for image-making—this has become widely used in the postmodern era.
- Discuss how the contemporary artist can use art to establish a critical dialogue with the past, and why critics cannot evaluate these artworks based on the older ideas of 'beauty' or 'aesthetics'.
- Explain how artists can use art as a critical tool to examine their own responses to the world. (8 marks)

11 Look at Plates 2, 3 and 4. Discuss how approaches to artworks change and vary over time.
- Discuss the difference between modernist and postmodernist approaches to artmaking.
- Acknowledge the differing uses of technology, and how these have changed the production of artworks.
- Explore the cultural significance and influence of each work. (8 marks)

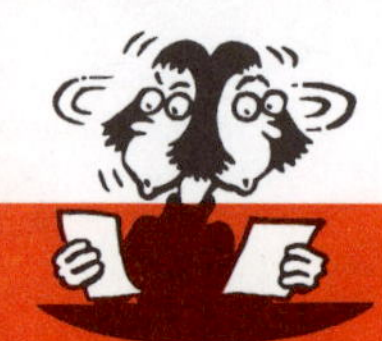

ANSWERS—KEY EXAM QUESTIONS

12 How have ideas about representation been conveyed in art through history? You must make reference to Plates 2, 3 and 4.

- Through history, the treatment of the same subject matter has changed (e.g. how the human form differs in each work over time).
- Different symbols and imagery have been used to represent dominant ideas of the time.
- The conventions, styles and materials used in artworks are relevant to the time of their production. (8 marks)

13 Critically analyse this artist's use of materials and his intentions in his artmaking. In your response make reference to Plates 5, 6 and 7.

- Text and image have been combined to communicate his ideas.
- McCahon uses modern paints, such as acrylic and polymers, rather than oils, which gives the works a more contemporary feel.
- There is a representation of spirituality which is not based on a specific religion. (12 marks)

14 Using Plates 5, 6 and 7, analyse how the artist is responding to his world. Make reference to possible meanings that can be associated with the artworks.

- McCahon explores the physical and spiritual qualities of his world.
- He constructs personal symbols and signs to convey deeply felt beliefs.
- He shows a stronger concern for the concepts of his subject matter, rather than a traditional artistic aesthetic—that is, he is responding to his world by conveying a specific message to his audience. (12 marks)

15 Using Plates 5, 6 and 7, examine what significant events may have influenced the artist and how these are represented in his artworks.

- The artist examines colonial issues concerning New Zealand.
- He explores the tradition of spirituality in art, offering an alternative genre to established religious art.
- We can see the impact of Christianity on the artist. (12 marks)

The following questions require extended-response answers that would take about 45 minutes to write. These are some ideas which may help you get started on the question(s) you choose to answer.

16 Explore the importance of issues and ideas to artists' approaches to art. Provide examples to support your response.

- The beliefs and ideas of the artist are paramount to the production of art. Traditional art was governed by conventions; modernism attacked these conventions in the form of the avant garde; and postmodernity critically addresses both the past and the present.
- Issues and events can stimulate the artist to produce works as a response of protest, or the opposite: compliance.

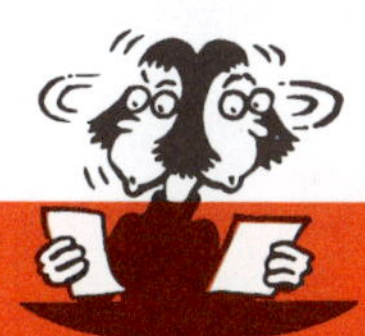

- Use examples from your case studies of artists who have produced works in response to particular ideas. Use strong examples which clearly show an idea or issue and the way each artist has responded. (25 marks)

17 Discuss how artists have interpreted their experiences through their artworks. Make reference to two or more artists you have studied.

- Artists use their artworks as forms of expression that outline their feelings and perceptions of their world, both physically and symbolically.
- The artworks act like diaries of their personal experiences and provide and insight into the perception of the artist's world.
- Use examples from your case studies which clearly show a relationship between the world of an artist and the artwork itself. They might, for example, include works which make reference to particular public events such as wars, political events or social changes, or to private events in the artist's life. (25 marks)

18 'Art critics provide the audience with a richer understanding of the artist's work.' Evaluate this statement and discuss the importance of the critic in visual arts. Support your response by making reference to artists and critics you have studied.

- In this answer, you need to *evaluate* the statement (do you agree?) and then *discuss* the importance of the role of the critic (e.g. explain how critics provide a richer understanding of art, and to whom).
- If you agree, for example, you might argue that the critic has specialist knowledge of artworks—their use of signs and symbols, use of technology and the philosophies or intentions of specific artists. These will provide a richer understanding of an artist's work for an audience who may not be able to see these aspects of an artwork.
- You could argue that the critic acts as a conduit (a 'connector') between the artwork and audience, providing a bridge between them so artworks can be understood by audiences. They can explain the meaning of signs and symbols which may be unknown to the audience.
- Use examples from your case studies of critics who have been instrumental in the appreciation of certain artists' works, e.g. Max Kozloff who championed pop art and the work of Andy Warhol.
- If you want to disagree with the statement, be very careful to back up your answer with plenty of examples. In this case, you might benefit from a balanced response which shows how critics can both provide a richer understanding, but also have the potential to mislead or confuse an audience. Make sure you use good case studies! (25 marks)

19 Explain how critics construct meaning in an artwork. Provide examples that support your explanation in your response.

- In this question, you need to know about the *process* of art criticism. How do critics look at artworks to find meaning in them? Have a look back on page 22 for the list of things a good critic needs to do.
- Critics use contextual information about an artwork. They look at when, where and how it was produced, and will use their knowledge of other artworks for comparison.

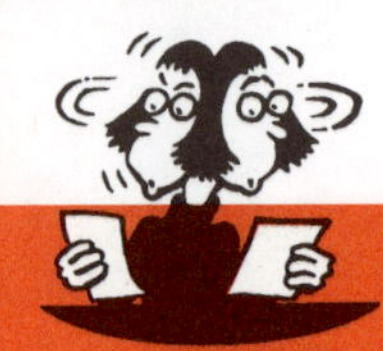

- Critics seek out the conceptual strength and meaning that is found in artworks. They then investigate the conventions that have been used, the modes of representation, and how the artist has expressed their ideas.
- You could use examples of how certain critics have been able to construct meaning in difficult or intricate works. (25 marks)

20 Discuss how historical studies have provided a better understanding of the practice of visual arts. In your response, provide examples of artwork you have studied to support your answer.
- Historical studies *contextualise* (locate in a time and place) the influential features that surround the production of an artwork.
- Art history provides a clearer insight into how a work was produced by researching the circumstances of the relevant time and place and giving an understanding of the art movements of the time.
- A knowledge of the technologies that were available at the time of the artwork provides a better insight into the artist's use of materials and development of techniques.
- You might use examples from your case studies of works that you understood more fully after you had studied the historical aspects of the era in which it was produced. How did art history help you understand how these works were produced? Why is this kind of knowledge important? (25 marks)

21 'It is impossible to relive the past.'
Evaluate this statement in terms of the historical value of artists and artworks you have studied.
- An artwork is an artefact of the past. It provides a 'window' which allows the audience to witness something about the artist and the conditions of the time in which it was produced.
- We cannot 'relive' the past, but artworks of the past provide a conceptual representation of what has occurred and the ideas of another period.
- You might use examples of artists who present powerful images from the past which bring history alive for you. We cannot 'relive' the past, but images in artworks can certainly evoke powerful emotional responses in us and cause us to experience what the artist wants us to experience of their history. (25 marks)

THE CONCEPTUAL FRAMEWORK—AGENCIES IN THE ARTWORLD

Page 40

1 Explain how the influences of the world can be seen in Plate 1.
- Depiction of a religious event—in this case, the Last Supper of Christ—shows the importance of Christianity and Christian imagery in the artmaking of this period.
- The use of formal elements such as balance and composition, and the use of perspective in the background, highlight the development of artistic conventions during the Renaissance. (4 marks)

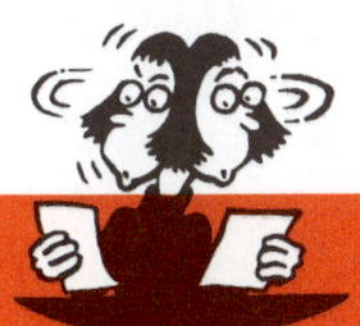

ANSWERS—KEY EXAM QUESTIONS

2 Who is the intended audience for Plate 1? Why?

- The scale (size) and placement of the artwork as a mural suggests that the intended audience was a mass public audience. The artist is intending public interaction with the artwork.
- The setting is based on a religious event, so presumably the audience would have been Christians attending church. (4 marks)

3 Describe the relationship between the audience and artist as seen in Plates 2 and 3.

- The artworks promote the idea that the artist is a protester and social critic of the times. Dix examines the social condition of Germany, whilst Kruger examines important issues for women.
- The artists provide personal insights into the social and political conditions of the time and provoke a personal response from the audience. (8 marks)

4 Give an account of how the artists respond to the world in Plates 2 and 3.

- Both artists attempt to provide an insight into the social conditions and issues of the time. Dix provides a graphic account of the victims of war, specifically World War I, while Kruger alerts the audience to the issues of rights for women (the body as a 'battleground' referring to the debates and controversy over issues such as abortion and eating disorders).
- The artists use their artworks as 'social diaries' to provide visual accounts of their experiences. Their intentions are to reveal what they see and feel in the world. (8 marks)

5 Look at Plates 4, 5 and 6 and the text extract, and comment on the importance of the relationship between the audience and the artwork.

- Andy Warhol's artworks use images of the everyday—they appear in popular media such as newspapers and cinema. By using familiar images, Warhol is making part of his work recognisable to the 1960s audience.
- The artist is keenly aware of how society is linked to the acceptance and appreciation of artworks.
- The artworks highlight the 'banality' (triviality, dullness) of consumer society (200 soup cans!). These were images the audience would have recognised, and which Warhol *wanted* the audiences to recognise.
- The artworks also provide today's audience with a sense of the 1960s. (13 marks)

6 Analyse how the artist has explored his world through his artworks, referring to Plates 4, 5 and 6.

- Warhol explores the everyday qualities of his world, ranging from the images of advertising to movie posters and newspaper articles.
- He has blurred the distinction between 'high-brow' and 'low-brow' art by using these everyday objects (as Duchamp did earlier in the twentieth century with his 'readymades').
- By using the process of silkscreen printing, he is exploring an everyday technique in an artistic way. (13 marks)

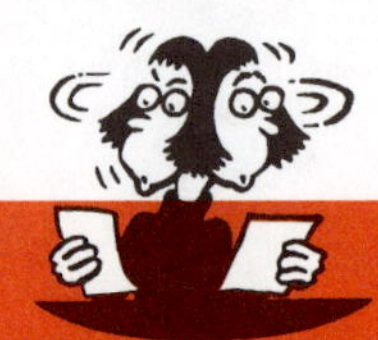

ANSWERS—KEY EXAM QUESTIONS

The following questions require extended-response answers that would take about 45 minutes to write. These are some ideas which may help you get started on the question(s) you choose to answer.

7 Select two or more artists you have studied and explain how they sought to change the world through their art.

- For this question, you might choose two similar artists, from a similar period of time or who explored similar themes, or choose two different artists and contrast how they wanted to change the world. Either way, establishing some link between them (whether it be a similarity or a contrast) will be helpful in structuring your response.
- Artists develop distinctive viewpoints and account for them in a particular visual manner which highlights the importance of style, technology, values and beliefs.
- Did your chosen artists want to change the world's ideas about art, or did they try to effect a greater social or political change? What did they want to change? What artistic conventions or styles did they use to do it? Were they successful?
- The role of the artist has changed greatly over time. For instance, Renaissance artists differ greatly from Romantic, modernist or even postmodernist artists. Artists have been great social or political activists, but this is not always the case. You should consider the state of the world the artists wanted to change. What did they think was wrong with their worlds? (25 marks)

8 'Art has nothing to do with the physical world. It is purely a product of the imagination of the artists.' Do you agree? Discuss, giving reasons for your answer.

- This comment suggests that the 'real world' has no influence on the artist. The question is asking if artists create their works in a vacuum or bubble, without any reference to the worlds they live in. Do you agree with this?
- If you disagree, you need to provide examples from your case studies of artworks which clearly reflect the world. You might even know examples of artists who have *claimed* that they are not interested in the world, but whose works clearly reflect it.
- The imagination of artists is, of course, very important, as it determines *how* the world will be depicted in the artworks.
- So your argument might be, for example, that the imagination of the artist is significant in the way the artist constructs their artworks, but there is still always an element of interaction between the artist and the world. (25 marks)

THE FRAMES

Page 53

1 How important is the imagination of the artist in Plate 1?

- The imaginative qualities in this image are important. The work synthesises personal and cultural symbols to create new meanings in a unique way.
- The use of recognised images such as Van Gogh's painting of the bedroom in Arles, *The Bedroom*, and the headless Australian Aboriginal highlights the clash of cultures and ideas in a dramatic way. (5 marks)

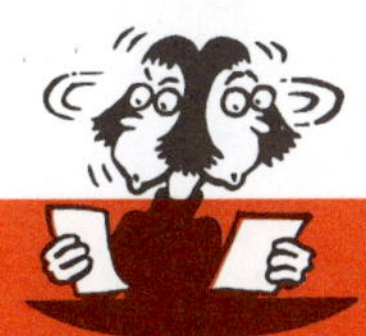

ANSWERS—KEY EXAM QUESTIONS

2 Discuss the effectiveness of the visual structure of the artwork in Plate 1.
- The artist uses familiar images from the history of art to construct a new and dramatic image. Each component in the painting references important aspects associated with the artist's perception of his world.
- The merging of differing styles and cultural symbols demonstrates the artist's ability to produce an artwork that deals with racial issues without being didactic ('preachy').

(5 marks)

3 How does Plate 1 construct a view of the society in which the artist lives?
- This work examines key issues concerning indigenous Australian culture and its assimilation into Western values and beliefs.
- The use of visual signs such as the bloody handprints, ceremonial costume and body painting juxtaposed (put next to) with the Western setting suggests that the artist lives in a time where there is a cultural tension between European/white Australian and Aboriginal peoples. (5 marks)

4 How important is the technique of *appropriation* to Plate 1?
- The use of appropriation in this work highlights the dominance of western images in Australia and articulates the violent process of assimilation in a pictorial and conceptual manner. It is of crucial importance.
- The use of recognisable imagery and sources such as Van Gogh's *The Bedroom* (1889), Greek sculpture and stencilled handprints provides a sense of familiarity yet, in this format, seems out of place. This makes the audience ask questions about why the images are juxtaposed in this way, and creates a dramatic image. (5 marks)

5 Compare and contrast the different personal depictions of the same setting in Plates 2 and 3.
- Meere's depiction is modernist, revealing a personal insight into an idealised society. Zahalka's work is postmodern and critically assesses Meere's depiction of Australian life.
- Meere's is a painting, whilst Zahalka's is a studio-based photograph.
- Both are constructed settings of natural leisure scenes, highlighting the personal view of both of the artists.
- Both works provide a sense of place at a particular time. (8 marks)

6 Look at Plates 2 and 3. Evaluate the different uses of media in each, and explain briefly how they are developed in the artworks.
- Meere's *Australian Beach Pattern* is a oil painting in which the human figure is idealised and the facial features of all the figures are repeated throughout the composition, suggesting a type of homogenous social identity to the subject matter.
- Zahalka constructs her setting in a studio, making the audience aware of its artificial staging and composition.
- Meere's painting creates a rhythmic energy in which the eye moves fluidly over the composition. Zahalka's photograph presents a static composition, which allows for greater scrutiny of the individuals in the work. (8 marks)

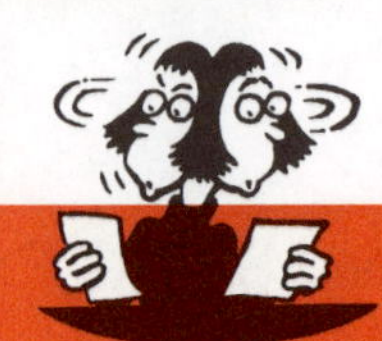

ANSWERS—KEY EXAM QUESTIONS

7 Discuss how visual codes and conventions are used in artworks, referring to Plates 2 and 3 in your answer.

- Both works constructs icons of Australian culture, but Zahalka's work is postmodernist in nature, while Meere's is modernist.
- Meere constructs a composition which is flowing and dynamic. The depiction of the figures, while varied, makes them all appear stylised and similar, suggesting a 'sameness' about them. The depiction of the figures is reminiscent of the idealised forms of neo-classical art, which used idealised figurative forms to represent beauty.
- Zahalka critically examines the issue of artificiality and constructed narratives. Her photograph uses models from diverse cultural backgrounds as a sign for cultural diversity in a postmodern world.
- Meere utilises traditional pictorial conventions in the construction of this painting. There is a flowing visual pathway, energetic use of line and colour and a celebration of the human form.
- Zahalka employs contemporary photographic techniques, which challenge the 'truthfulness' of the photograph and provided greater opportunity to scrutinise the identity of the subjects depicted. (8 marks)

8 What do the two works tell the audience about the treatment of race and gender in art?

- Meere's treatment of race and gender is one that constructs uniformity. The issue of class is difficult to discern, since the scene depicts leisure activities, yet even in this situation there is a monumental quality to the depiction of the figures in the painting. Zahalka is keenly aware of the way the audience scrutinises cultural diversity, so her treatment of the race and gender of the subjects is more naturalistic rather than the idealised forms ('national identities') created by Meere.
- Meere constructs an idealised view of Australian culture, which is entrenched in traditional Western representations of the human form. Zahalka offers a more critical account of the subject matter. (8 marks)

9 *Irony* and *appropriation* are two key conventions within postmodern art. Discuss these in reference to Plates 2 and 3.

- Appropriation has been employed as a strategy by artists who question the traditions and expectation of artists from previous periods. In postmodern art, it involves taking an image or object and using it in a new context, encouraging the audience to see it in a new light and critically analyse it. Anne Zahalka clearly uses appropriation here to question the presentation of idealised Australia in Charles Meere's *Australian Beach Pattern*.
- Zahalka also employs irony in *The Bathers*—rather than realistically depicting the setting, Zahalka obviously constructs an artificial setting in a very 'tongue-in-cheek' manner. It suggests a different cultural heritage to that of Meere and, in being artificially constructed itself, makes an ironic comment on the unreality of Meere's version of Australian society. (8 marks)

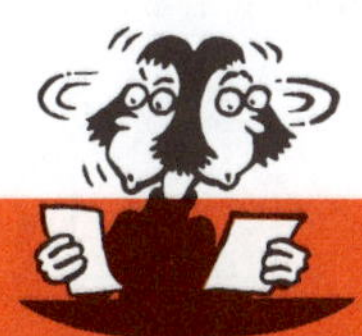

ANSWERS—KEY EXAM QUESTIONS

10 Investigate the significance of personal perception in the artist's approach to artmaking. Refer to Plates 4, 5 and 6 and the text in your answer.

- Each artist, through their own style, provides a personal, visual account of the human form.
- The development of the style can be associated with historical development in art, as the text extract suggests.
- Each artist invites the viewer to participate in their constructed world and creates a presence. Ingres seeks to create a seductive setting in which the female acknowledges and invites the viewer into her world. De Kooning provides a different account of the figure in which the gestural brush strokes and piercing gaze confront the viewer. Sharpe confronts the view with a different perception of the female figure which is powerful and dynamic. (12 marks)

11 Look at Plates 4, 5 and 6 and the text. Examine the way each artist constructs artworks, considering their formal qualities, style and intention.

- Ingres: uses a theatrical setting, refined paint application, creating a realistic and inviting figure who draws the gaze of the viewer.
- De Kooning: uses linear, grotesque, dynamic, discordant colours. This painting is unsettling and confronts the audience with a disquieting physical presence.
- Sharpe: this work is lyrical, expressive, eclectic and confronts the viewer with a sense of self-confidence (it is a self-portrait) of the subject.
- The artworks demonstrate the development of visual conventions, ranging between the realism of Ingres, the expressionistic approach of De Kooning and the conceptual interplay of Sharpe. (12 marks)

12 What significance has gender played upon the artist's approach to artmaking? Refer to Plates 4, 5 and 6 and the text in your answer.

- All three artists are dealing with the female form, highlighting this as the dominant nude form in the Western tradition.
- We can see differences in the gaze of the subjects on the audience.
- Ingres: the gaze is one of comfort and docility, reflecting the role of women and the conceptions of beauty in Ingres' time.
- De Kooning: the gaze is more anxious here, reflecting the role of women in the 1950s.
- Sharpe: a defiant gaze can be seen in Sharpe's self-portrait, reflecting a picture of later twentieth century feminism.
- Each image, therefore, may highlight the social value of women in each period of time. (12 marks)

13 Look at Plates 4, 5 and 6 and the text. How can the artworks be reinterpreted by a contemporary audience?

- Treatment of the female form by male artists (Ingres, de Kooning) differs greatly to that of the female artist (Sharpe). A contemporary audience, with the benefit of hindsight, can look at the historical conditions and assess the treatment of the subject.

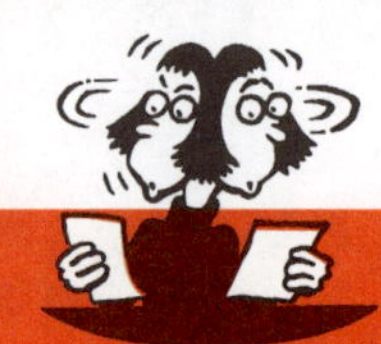

ANSWERS—KEY EXAM QUESTIONS

- In light of theories such as feminism and postmodernism, a contemporary audience can look at the first two depictions of the female form and note the lack of power the women seem to display, and compare that to Wendy Sharpe's.
- A contemporary audience can critically assess the idea that the female form was seen, historically, as a commodity—something to be owned, like a painting. Through postmodernism, this idea is being challenged. (12 marks)

The following questions require extended-response answers that would take about 45 minutes to write. These are some ideas which may help you get started on the question(s) you choose to answer.

14 Evaluate the importance of personal values and beliefs in the works of artists you have studied. Give examples of artworks to support your response.

- This is an *evaluate* question, which means you have to 'weigh up' the importance of the artist's personal values and beliefs in creating artworks. Is it very important? Not very important? Either way, you have to use examples to back up your point of view.
- If you think personal beliefs are very important, you could discuss artworks that have been vehicles for the personal expression of artists and describe how the emotional state of the artist has dictated the treatment and form used. You'll need to select and discuss artworks that demonstrate significant emotional qualities.
- If you choose to argue that personal beliefs and values are *not* very important, you'll need good, solid examples to back up your argument. (25 marks)

15 How has spirituality been an important source for artists you have studied? Give examples of artworks to support your response.

- Select and discuss artworks that deal with varying forms of personal belief and spirituality. Remember there are many different kinds of spirituality that can be expressed in art, and using a good mix of examples will help you structure your essay. 'Spirituality' does not necessarily refer to only organised religions like Christianity or Islam.
- You should examine how personal beliefs have been a motivational force in the production of art, and could even discuss how spirituality has established genres in religious art. (25 marks)

16 'Form or structure can be the most important element in an artwork.'
Discuss, referring to two or more artists you have studied.

- For this question, you should select and discuss artists who demonstrate effective use of formal qualities—signs, symbols, conventions, codes—in their artmaking. How does the structure of the works give them their meaning?
- Highlight how different artists over periods of time will establish particular visual conventions that demonstrate a specific interest in the development of the structure of the artwork. Using two or more contrasting artists might be useful here. (25 marks)

17 'Artworks operate within specific codes and conventions that convey meaning.'
Do you agree? Refer to artworks that you have studied in your answer.

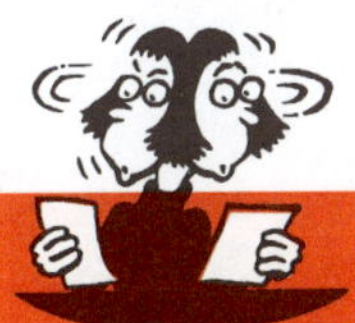

ANSWERS—KEY EXAM QUESTIONS

- It is unlikely you will disagree with this statement! The main issue is to provide specific examples from your case studies of the different kinds of 'codes and conventions' artists use.
- You will also need to clearly define what you understand by the concept of 'codes and conventions'.
- How does an audience get meaning and understand the artist's ideas in an artwork by identifying these conventions and signs?
- Discuss how artists will employ public and private symbols to communicate to an audience. **(25 marks)**

18 How have artworks reflected the spirit of a time and place? Make specific reference to artworks you have studied.

- First, you need to define the terms of the question. What is the 'spirit of a time and place'? This is a question about the cultural frame you have studied. It is asking you how artworks reflect the culture of a particular place and era.
- Artworks comment upon the ideas and values of the time in which they are produced. They become artefacts that provide an insight into the culture and society.
- They can make clear social or political comments, or simply reflect something of the culture through their subject matter or techniques. The use of technology can signal when an artwork was produced. Digital technologies, for example, reflect something of our contemporary age.
- Use examples where the 'spirit' of an era has been displayed in artworks. **(25 marks)**

19 Analyse how artists employ systems of signs and symbols to convey ideas about culture and society.

- There are two distinct parts of this question. The first is that artists use signs and symbols, and the second is that they use these to convey ideas about the society around them.
- Signs and symbols are culturally specific and are understood in particular ways according to the cultural identity of the audience.
- Look at the difference between Western and Eastern traditions, for example: there are very different cultural perceptions, and different signs(s)ymbols are used. You might find it helpful to use examples of artists who come from very different cultural backgrounds, or from different time periods.
- Artists will employ particular symbols to convey their ideas. Some artists use the same symbols in their work. Remember that ideas about culture will vary over time as well as place. **(25 marks)**

20 How has postmodern art sought to redefine the world?

- Postmodern artists review the legitimacy of dominant cultures and histories which tend to exclude minority groups. Through their art, postmodern artists challenge and critique this process of marginalisation. This is a way of 'redefining' the world.
- The constant employment of new and hybridised (fused or mixed) art forms, technologies, ideas and media all assist in the artist and audience reevaluating the world and the techniques of creating art.

- Use examples of postmodern artists and, if possible, earlier artists whose work is critiqued by the postmodern artists. If you can show this kind of comparison, it will display your knowledge more widely. (25 marks)

21 How important is irony in art? Discuss, making reference to specific artworks you have studied.

- The question is asking you how important irony is in artworks you have studied. This would be a question you would only tend to answer if you agreed that irony is very important.
- Irony calls into question the legitimacy of the artwork, artist and audience, making the audience question the way they are seeing and interpreting an artwork. This makes it an important tool for both artists and audiences.
- Irony is a strategy used historically and in a contemporary context to undermine dominant structures. Postmodern artists employ it construct a critical dialogue with the subject matter.
- Use examples of artworks in which irony is a central and defining feature, where irony conveys the artwork's meaning. (25 marks)

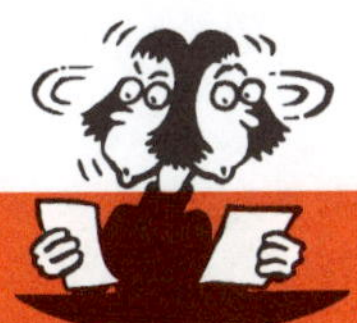

ANSWERS—SAMPLE HSC EXAMINATION PAPER

The answers provided here are simply point-form guidelines for your answers; yours may, of course, differ from these. You need to keep in mind the marks allocated for each type of question and adjust the length of your answers accordingly. You should use full sentences, not point form, in your own answers. The extended-response question you choose should be answered in full essay format.

SECTION I—Pages 74–77

Question 1

- He uses a highly stylised rather than naturalistic realism.
- The use of the traditional medium of bronze suggests that the artist is interested in extending the language of sculpture in a more imaginative manner.
- The solid mass present generates a presence, expressed through the artist's interpretation of the human form. (5 marks)

Question 2

- Each image depicts women in activities of everyday life. The images suggest the subjects are unaware of being viewed, which portrays a very naturalistic setting.
- All the images reveal an intimate scene. Morisot shows the loving activities of a mother, Millet communicates to the audience a sense of a time and place before industrialisation, whilst Gauguin provides a visual account of another culture very different from that of 1890s Europe.
- The artworks document everyday life and show the power of art to translate this in marvellous ways. They provide an intimate insight into private, everyday lives rather than grandiose or public events.
- Each image reflects a romantic natural realism of the nineteenth century. (8 marks)

Question 3

- The artwork is a collaborative work between indigenous and western artists in which a dialogue with the past is established and the spirit of making the artwork reflects the desire for reconciliation.
- The use of the poles to tell stories and provide verbal and accounts of the past highlights the importance of history to inform and stimulate the artmaking.
- The artwork examines the historical narratives that have been developed by the European colonisers and the indigenous culture.
- The artists use materials which are historically specific to the area around the Museum.
- The installation appears at the entrance of the Museum of Sydney (which traces the history of Sydney), highlighting the importance of history to contemporary society.
- The work is postmodern in term of its reassessment of the past actions of European colonisers. (12 marks)

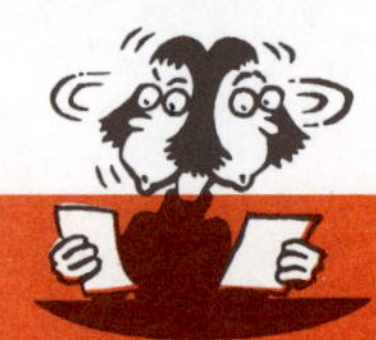

ANSWERS—SAMPLE HSC EXAMINATION PAPER

SECTION II—Pages 78–79

Question 4

This is an example of a response to this question by a student, Elizabeth Jo. The question is worth 25 marks.

A central thinking of artists is to employ a visual strategy to critique, as well as reflect, the political ideologies of their times. In essence their artmaking is propelled by the central idea of critiquing their times. Modernist John Heartfield (born Helmut Herzfeld, 1891–1968) was a German artist renowned for his agitprop-style photomontages and his role in the development of the politically orientated Dada movement in Berlin. Heartfield's work critiqued the emergence of the Fascist ideology that grew to consume Europe, particularly during World War II in works such as 'Adolf the Superman Swallows Gold and Spouts Junk' (1932) and 'Hurrah, the Butter is Gone!' (1935). Comparably within a postmodern context, contemporary Chinese artist and activist Ai Weiwei (b. 1957) orientates conceptual concerns, employing his artworks as a platform to critically analyse the current Communist Chinese Government's stance on democracy and human rights, as seen in works such as 'Study of Perspective Tiananmen Square' (1995) and 'Straight' (2008–12). Hence both artists from respective times and places are driven by the central idea of art as a tool for political expression and a mechanism that can critique governments and their actions. Both Heartfield and Weiwei resonate personal concerns through a visual critique that is shaped by their central thoughts on the zeitgeist of their respective cultural and historical contexts.

The social circumstance of Europe drastically shifted with the demise of the Weimar Republic in Germany. The rise of the National Socialist Party (Nazi party) generated a false consciousness that would allow them to become a repressive state. Marxist theorist Louis Althusser would later title this type of regime as a repressive state apparatus. The Nazi regime sought to homogenise social and ethical values that would historically prove to be at the cost of humanity. Heartfield felt that the ideological shift was irreconcilable and sought to critically review this event through his art, and also reflect the demise of social sensibilities in Germany at the time. As with most of the German Dadaists, such as George Groz and Hannah Hoch, Heartfield ensured his art was motivated by political expression. To aid his practice, irony and absurdist iconography fuelled by the conceptual concerns of the Dadaist manifesto forged Heartfield's artistic intent. Employing the photomontage, Heartfield transmuted the images that populated the media of the time and created critical visual hybrids that denounced the rise of Adolf Hitler and the repressive state apparatus of the Nazi party. His art was a mirror of the social turmoil of the time: an aesthetic positioned within Dadaist intentions and positions in a left-wing context, most of his photomontages regularly appeared in the German Communist Party magazine AIZ. Heartfield manipulated a medium associated with truth values to present jarring truths of German society that were often rendered invisible. His innovative avant-garde approach to photography demonstrated his innovation of material and the complex use of symbols to present imagery of agitation. Ascribed to Marxist theories his artworks were driven by the desire to provoke the audience to consider the social conditions of the time.

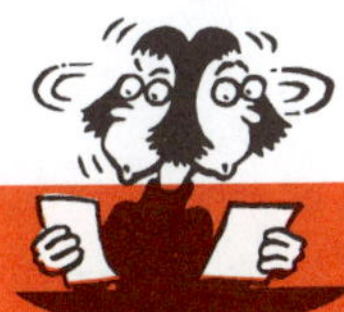

'The most aggressive political use of photomontage was in the work of John Heartfield, who … brought it to a pitch of polemical ferocity that no artist has since equalled' (Robert Hughes). In 'Adolf the Superman Swallows Gold and Spouts Junk,' Heartfield exposes the contradiction between Hitler's anti-capitalist rhetoric and his pro-capitalist practices. The photomontage technique allows the artist to create a satirical image by combining different photographs: a portrait of Hitler; an X-ray of a human body; a vertebral column of gold coins and the insignia of the Nazi party; and a swastika placed over his heart. The title, in conjunction with the image of the X-ray, is a metaphor referring to the large contributions that wealthy industrialists were making to the Nazi Party (National Socialist German Worker's Party) despite its alleged basis in socialism. Heartfield's image reveals the contradictions between Hitler's financial support and his workingman rhetoric.

Heartfield's 'Hurrah, the Butter is Gone!' (1935) is a satirical anti-Fascist photomontage that challenges Hermann Göring (German politician and leading member of the Nazi Party). This work is a parody of a speech by Göring, a quote from which is included at the bottom of the image. It reads: 'Ore has always made an empire strong, butter and lard have made a country fat at most.' Göring, who was responsible for the industrial and military rearmament of the country, repeatedly demanded an increase in the iron industry's productive capacity to boost the exploitation of domestic ores. The quote used in this work, which stems from a 1935 speech in Hamburg, is an example of the aggressive, militarist rhetoric Göring employed to convince Germans of the necessity of making sacrifices for the country's rearmament—even if this entailed food shortages. Heartfield's montage portrays a typical German family, whose patriotism and loyalty to the Nazis is illustrated by several details: the Hitler portrait; the swastika-patterned wallpaper; the sofa cushion bearing Hindenburg's likeness; and the framed verse in the upper left—'Lieb Vaterland magst ruhig sein' ('Dear Fatherland, no danger thine'), which stems from the 19th-century patriotic song 'Die Wacht am Rhein' (The Watch on the Rhine). In their blind loyalty to the Führer, this family appears to have forgotten that iron is no substitute for food and instead cheers 'Hurrah, the butter is gone!'. Thus Heartfield challenges the unquestioning loyalty of the Nazi party's supporters, even though it is detrimental to their everyday life.

While there has been an ideological shift from modernism to postmodernism, contemporary artists still employ their art as a tool of social expression presenting the core concept that artworks should provoke sociopolitical advocacy. Ai Weiwei is an artist who, like Heartfield, seeks to critique the repression of the Chinese Communist state. He presents through his art a penetrating mirror of the social conditions of a government and land that is subjugated and harshly controlled. His practice adapts a post-Dadaist approach that evocatively presents issues and ideas that challenge the social norms of contemporary China. His post-Duchampian use of material and his indebtedness to German Dadaist political expression allows Ai Weiwei to produce artworks that use unique material in an evocative manner to reflect the values and beliefs of contemporary China. His work has its roots in both the political agitation of Dada as well as the aesthetic concerns of contemporary Chinese artists' groups such as the Star Group and art movements such as Political Pop and Cynical Realism.

Ai challenges the Chinese government in his photograph 'Study of Perspective Tiananmen

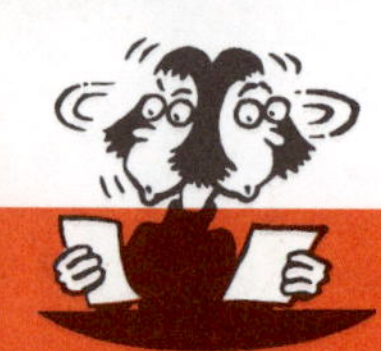

Square' (38.9 x 59 cm). In what first appears to be a classic tourist snapshot, Ai sticks his middle finger up at Tiananmen Square Gate. Also known as the 'Gate of Heavenly Peace', and formerly the front entrance to the Forbidden City, this was also the site of the brutal massacre in 1989 in which state soldiers shot peaceful protesters. The Beijing government still refuses to discuss it and censors all footage of the event. 'Study of Perspective Tiananmen Square' was part of a series begun in 1995 and completed in 2003. The Eiffel Tower in Paris, The Reichstag in Berlin and the White House in Washington DC all receive the same treatment in these parodies of 'Renaissance perspective'. The central rule that objects closer to the eye must appear larger is being used to showcase an offensive gesture expressing Ai's disdain for state power, which is by no means limited to China. In its resemblance to 'Tank Man', an unidentified protestor photographed in 1989 facing a line of tanks, Ai's finger, standing alone against symbols of state power at the centre of this image, is a provocative stand-in for a figure strictly banned in the Chinese media, and therefore truly provocative. Hence Ai critiques the government's censorship of a major event in their history, which impinges upon the artist's personal belief in democracy. The central idea of truth, social justice and authentic existence are the key ideas that are motivating his art practice.

Both a stylized representation of an earthquake and an image of its effects, 'Straight' (1200 x 600 cm) is a statement about a specific instance of governmental corruption and negligence. The province of Sichuan suffered massive casualties in an earthquake of 2008, leaving 90 000 dead or missing. Over 5000 were children killed when poorly constructed schools collapsed on top of them. Ai, a self-taught architect, was outraged to discover that this could have been avoided. Both a memorial and a call to action, 'Straight' is part of the artist's broader effort to hold the Chinese government accountable and urge it to take preventative steps to avoid future disaster. The monumental sculptural instillation consists of the bent and broken steel reinforcement bars that were part of the poorly constructed schools. He commissioned metal workers to straighten and mend them until they looked as they would have before the earthquake. He arranged the bars in waves that resemble the oscillations in an earthquake on a seismograph, while the fissures between them resemble fault lines. The thousands of individual components symbolise the individual lives lost, demanding that the audience visualises and considers the causalities rather than merely reading a statistic. The installation adopted an aesthetic form similar to the minimal sculptures and installation of Richard Serra and later of Maya Lin, but transmuted minimalist philosophy for a more didactic message about the earthquake and the loss of life. Ai Weiwei effectively attacked the Chinese government's failings and resonated the issues to a transglobal community. His use of material and a culturally contextual semiology ensured national attention was drawn to the event and marked the beginning of a turbulent period in Ai's adversarial relationship with Chinese authorities. This artwork critically deconstructs the failings of a government to address social and ethical concerns. Ai's work seeks to unpick the ideological superstructure of China, exposing the constructed worldview of the state apparatus, acknowledging its repressive actions and questionable practices. Ai's conceptual concern is to expose the state's bias and lack of value for human rights.

Ultimately both John Heartfield and Ai Weiwei effectively articulate the idea of producing artworks as powerful critical accounts of their ideological position in their respective societies. Modernist Heartfield employs Dadaist aesthetics that were contemplative and conceptual

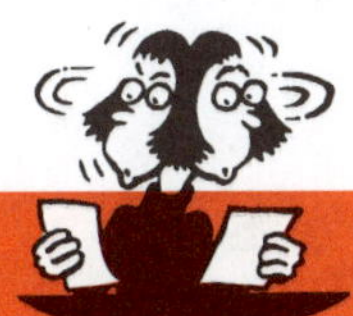

rather than pleasing to the eye in order to comment on the rise of the National Socialist Party in Weimar Germany. Central to this was the idea rather than the aesthetic experience. His iconography was aggressive and sought to agitate the audience, presenting a left-wing perspective of a repressive moment in Germany's history in which it was dangerous to offer any variation of the dominant viewpoint. His art was forged by the Dadaist concerns to deconstruct bourgeois ideologies and caustically demonstrate the barbarity of the Nazi party. Comparably, Postmodernist Ai Weiwei utilised a similar aesthetic strategy some 80 years later. Rather than attacking the Nazi Party, however, Ai identified and criticised the Chinese Communist Party and its stance on democracy and human rights. Both artists employed political ideas in their artworks as both aesthetic and ideological tools to critique the values of their respective times. Their art is conceptually driven to be both a mirror to reflect social concerns as well as a microscope to make the public aware of the repressive system of the respective governments. These artists offer an insight into the social and political settings of the time and consciously enlist their artwork in the service of social change.

Question 5

- This question requires you to look at different time periods and the kinds of artmaking practices which have been used. Your examples should come from a number of different periods of time to illustrate this.
- New technologies have changed artmaking over time and given more scope for experimentation as time has progressed.
- Prevailing ideas about the *purpose* of art have changed over time: e.g. spiritual purposes, secular (non-spiritual) purposes, social critique, political commentary and so on.
- Changing ideologies have changed the way art is produced.
- As artists review past styles and use or reject them, so artmaking practice changes.
- The different conditions surrounding artists change the practice too. How have the financial aspects of being an artist changed the way they work? (25 marks)

Question 6

- This question is asking about the role of the audience in the artworld. How does the audience ensure that art can exist?
- You need to define what you mean by the audience: general public, critics, historians, students, teachers ... all of these groups can be defined as the 'audience' of art.
- The audience is the critical consumer of art.
- Note the importance of patronage—people and institutions who fund artworks and artists—and the attendance of public exhibitions.
- Identify how artists aim to address specific audiences with their artworks. (25 marks)

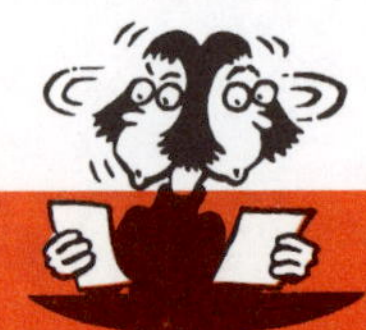

ANSWERS—SAMPLE HSC EXAMINATION PAPER

Question 7

This is an example of a response to this question by a student, Jessica Tyrrell.
This question is worth 25 marks.

Artists use the world around them as a stimulus and the basis to reflect the concerns and issues of their time; the world in which artists operate in is inexorably linked to their artmaking. It is interesting to compare the way that two completely different art movements—Abstraction and Pop Art—were both representations of the artists' experiences, class, ideology, age and significant events.

Abstraction was an artistic movement that appeared between the two World Wars and reflected the artists' growing disillusionment with society as a response to the tumultuous events at the beginning of the twentieth century—the World Wars, the Russian Revolution and the Weimar Republic in Germany. Alienated by the horrors of these events and also the materialism of modernity, many artists turned into themselves for spiritual enlightenment through artistic expression.

Where World War I caused the Dadaists to reject rationality and pursue a nihilistic worldview, the Abstractionists, in two different but parallel movements—Abstract Expressionism and Geometric Abstraction—became deeply spiritual and moved away from the notion of representation of figurative things to embrace representations of emotion.

Piet Mondrian and Kazimir Malevich were the leaders in Geometrical Abstraction: a movement in which pristine geometrical forms were meticulously arranged to form a perfect equilibrium between all the artistic elements. Mondrian's experiences of being brought up in a strict Calvinist Dutch village influenced his work greatly, in that he was constantly searching for pure spiritual experience through artistic expression. Malevich's upbringing also influenced his search for pure abstraction, as his massive works *White on White* seemed to echo the monumental Russian icons of his upbringing.

On the other side of the Abstractionists' spectrum were Wassily Kandinsky and Jackson Pollock. The Abstract Expressionists used a spontaneous manner to express themselves through art.

Kandinsky's Russian Orthodox upbringing and the mysticism of his childhood made him desire to express his spirituality through art. The son of two musicians, music would become a deep concern in his art, as he explored the relationship between music, colour and feelings. Like all the other European Abstractionists his work conveyed a theosophical yearning for transcendence of appearances to a deeply spiritual state.

Jackson Pollock was also deeply spiritual but his affinity was with nature and the American West. His investigations into the artistic practices of the Native American Navaho Indian sand painters led him to discover an entirely new method of painting. He let his body gestures influence where he dripped paint onto a horizontal canvas. He made deeply expressive and non-figurative paintings that echoed the spontaneity and exuberance of Kandinsky's dancing compositions.

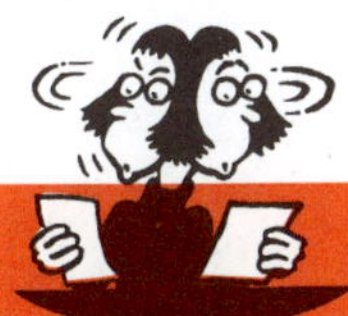

Relating to the disasters of the world in which they lived, the Abstractionists took various paths to find deep spiritual fulfilment through artistic expression. Because they were not making physical representations, they were free to focus on the personal and spiritual expression of colour, shape, line, direction and space. This marked a departure from a tradition as old as painting itself which represents figuratively the world of the artist; the artists were now abstractly representing their emotional response to their worlds.

In the 1950s and 60s a group of 'Pop Artists' reacted to what they saw as elitism in Abstract Expressionism. They worked to make a type of art that was representative of the consumer heaven of American postwar society and was easily accessible to the masses, just like mass advertising. Taking their cue from Duchamp's *LHOOQ,* they set out to mock all that was revered in western culture by making low culture into high art. This is a marked transgression within the artworld in terms of established aesthetic conventions; such artists set out to upset the audience's expectation of aesthetics and art practice in general.

Pop artists became 'aesthetic scavengers', turning the images they saw all around them in their world into art—Coke bottles, comic strips and fast food. This shows how the move towards capitalist consumerism in postwar America marked a complete turnaround in the way that artists saw their world. Pop Art created an iconography of popular taste and challenged the conditions of high art.

The most famous of the Pop Artists was Andy Warhol, who utilised a 'proto-postmodern' approach. He highlighted the employment of a commercial design process into a fine art context, producing screen prints ranging from images of Campbell's soup cans to car crashes, Marilyn Monroe and Mao Zedong which gave him international celebrity. Warhol used this idea of celebrity, a tenet of American popular culture, to simultaneously mock and pay homage to American society, where even people, it seemed, could become a commodity.

Warhol's practice echoed the nature of American society. He created an assembly line in his studio, which he called the Factory, again challenging the accepted notions of art practice within modernism. The process of printing artworks about soup cans became identical to the process in which these items were actually produced—on an assembly line.

By examining the way that the world affected two entirely different groups of artists, we can see that art does reflect the cultural and social interests in the world, and that these are always represented by artists in their artworks. The Abstractionists represented the disillusionment with society at the beginning of the 20th century and the Pop Artists represented the culture in which they lived after the world began to recover from these events.

Question 8

This is an example of a response written to this question by a student, Anjuli Maniam. This question is worth 25 marks.

Understanding the influence of culture on an individual's identity is a prime element in concluding a final meaning and an understanding of an artist's intentions. Culture, encompassing a particular social, spiritual and educational background, is invariably a factor

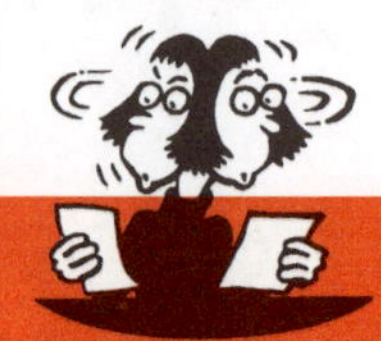

contributing to the communication of an artwork and its meaning. A major form of art which demonstrates a dependence on culture is Aboriginal art. All Aboriginal art, whether traditional or contemporary, provides many levels of meaning. Like most artworks, Aboriginal art presents a surface significance read by the system of signs and symbols. However, on a deeper layer, Aboriginal art also possesses a spiritual understanding, conceived through its cultural interpretation.

Traditional Indigenous artworks primarily focus on the depiction of events and stories about the Dreaming. The Dreaming is fundamental to Aboriginal culture as it is the spiritual dimension of existence which establishes the Aboriginal way of life. Through this cultural narrative, a new meaning is revealed in the artworks. For example, the common rock images of primordial spirits provide an understanding of the immanent and transcendent nature of creative forces within the environment. This Aboriginal belief—that the ancestral beings which created the world still dwell within the land—gives insight into the artists' intention to mark where a spirit withdrew from the physical world. For example, rock images of Wandjina, a creative force, signify where it has entered the earth.

In 1972 a government settlement in Alice Springs established an art co-op involving senior Indigenous men. The group, who are recognised as Papunya Tula, began the explosion in popularity of Aboriginal art in Australia. Through the use of semiology, the artists were able to communicate the cultural activities of their communities to the greater public and also transmit their cultural heritage through the generations in the form of art. Aboriginal spirituality is passed on through the generations of tribes by means of oral transmission. Oral discourses include dance, ceremonies, stories and art. This cultural knowledge of Indigenous communication additionally presents another of the artists' intentions.

The 'invisible culture' embodied in traditional Aboriginal art also resonates in contemporary works such as those by Tracey Moffatt and Gordon Bennett. Tracey Moffatt is an internationally acclaimed Aboriginal artist. Her culturally loaded images explore postcolonial issues of identity. Profoundly influenced by film and photography, Moffatt's work is said to resemble the conceptually rich artworks of Cindy Sherman. Moffatt's photographic series 'Something More' (1989) portrays Moffatt herself in rural landscapes. This piece investigates Moffatt's identity infused with her cultural background to convey historical events in Australia and the human conditioning exemplified through Indigenous Australians. Moffatt's self-awareness of her identity divulges a powerful narrative in which multiple perspectives and understandings of both artworks and artists' intentions can be deciphered.

Another contemporary Indigenous artist is Gordon Bennett. Bennett's work can be characterised through his infusion of both Indigenous and Western cultures to synthesise a new meaning. The prominent element of semiology as a communicator of culture creates authority and complexity in his artworks, which can be read in a multitude of narratives. For example, a common symbol used by Bennett in his artworks is the framework of linear perspective. Linear perspective, a highly recognised notion of Western art, signifies the scientific imperialism of the European culture in contrast to the spiritual perspective of Aboriginal peoples. Bennett also manipulates a range of other media in order to convey his meanings. One performance piece

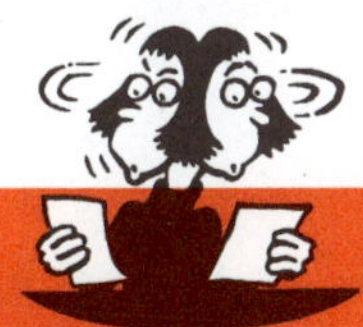

incorporates Bennett wrapped in white bandages violently whipping a black box of human size. This cultural definition and separation communicated through the contrasted colours of the black box and Bennett's white face represents the historic treatment of Indigenous Australians in the 19th century. Bennett's intention to communicate historic narratives is manipulated by marginalising and simplifying the cultural semiology of the artwork.

These various issues investigated by traditional and contemporary Indigenous artists of Australia are conveyed to the audience through the representation of cultural groups. Through the understanding of unique cultures, the viewer is able to analyse dissonant interpretations of the specific artwork in terms of its meaning and the artist's intentions. As a result, from these multiple perspectives one reaps a greater understanding of the artwork as a whole.

Question 9

- This question deals with the Postmodern Frame. You should be very familiar with the nature of postmodern art, and have studied in depth a number of postmodern artists, if you attempt this question.
- What conventions within art does postmodernism challenge? For example, the conventions of 'aesthetics' in art—the very nature of what art is—are questioned.
- Postmodernism also calls into question the legitimacy of 'originality' and the concept of 'artistic genius', which therefore also questions the role of the postmodern artist. Postmodern art suggests that the artist is far less important than the responses and interpretations of the audience.
- Postmodern art is anti-authoritarian and as a result questions all rights to the 'authority' of artists.
- You need to use examples of postmodern artists who have challenged conventions (and specifically name which conventions they are challenging) and discuss how they question their own legitimacy—that is, their own right be called 'artists' and produce artworks with a 'message' for an audience. (25 marks)

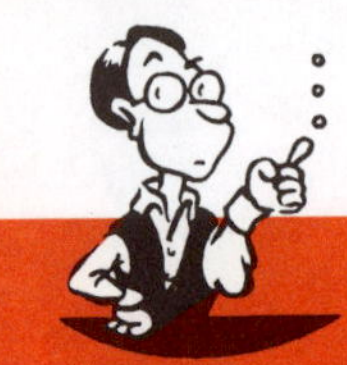

READING REFERENCE LIST

Reading difficulty: * Easy
** Moderate
*** Complex

General Texts

NSW Education Standards Authority, *Visual Arts Stage 6 Syllabus*
www.educationstandards.nsw.edu.au/wps/portal/nesa/11-12/Understanding-the-curriculum(s)yllabuses-a-z

** Feldman, Edmund Burke. *Varieties of Visual Experience*
Abrams, New York, 1992

* Hopwood, Graham. *Handbook of Art*
G. Hopwood, North Balwyn, 1974

** Marsh, Margaret et al. *ART: Art, Research and Theory*
Oxford University Press, Melbourne, 1999

** Sullivan, Graeme. *Seeing Australia: Views of Artists and Artwriters*
Piper Press, Sydney, 1994

* Aland, Jenny and Darby, Max. *Australian ArtLook*
Rigby Heinemann, Melbourne, 1997

Practice in Artmaking, Art Criticism & Art History

** Hoffert, Bernard. *Aesthetics and Art Criticism: the Role of Emotion in Art*
Longman, Melbourne, 1997

** Israel, Glenis. *Senior Artwise: Visual Arts 11–12*
Jacaranda Press, Milton (Vic), 2000

** Williams, Donald and Simpson, Colin. *Art Now: Contemporary Art Post–1970*
McGraw-Hill, Sydney, 1994

** Williams, Donald and Simpson, Colin. *Art Now: Contemporary Art Post–1970 (Book II)*
McGraw-Hill, Sydney, 1996

** Catalano, Gary. *Building a Picture: Interviews with Australian Artists*
McGraw-Hill, Sydney, 1997

** Harrison, Charles and Wood, Paul (eds). *Art in Theory, 1900–1990: An Anthology of Changing Ideas*
Blackwell, Oxford (UK), 1993

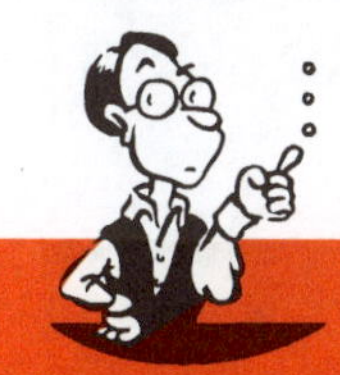

READING REFERENCE LIST

The Conceptual Framework–Agencies in the Artworld

** Marsh, Margaret et al. *ART: Art, Research and Theory*
Oxford University Press, Melbourne, 1999

** Hughes, Robert. *The Shock of the New: Art and the Century of Change*
BBC, London, 1980

** Hoffert, Bernard et al. *Art in Diversity*. (2nd ed)
Longman Australia, Melbourne, 1995

* Hoffert, Bernard. *Art Notes: Senior Study Guide*
Longman Cheshire, Melbourne, 1993

*** Gayford, Martin and Wright, Karen (eds). *The Penguin Book of Art Writing*
Viking, London, 1998

Frames

*** MacLachlan, Gale L. *Framing and Interpretation*
Melbourne University Press, Carlton, 1994

** Appignanesi, Richard. *Postmodernism for Beginners*
Icon Books, Cambridge, 1999

NOTES